Year 4/P5

Ann Montague-Smith

Text © Ann Montague-Smith 2002
Original illustrations © Nelson Thornes Ltd 2002

The right of Ann Montague-Smith to be identified as author of this work has been asserted by her in accordance with the Copyright, Designs and Patents Act 1988.

All rights reserved. The copyright holders authorise ONLY users of *Assess and Review Year 4/P5* to make photocopies of the resource sheets for their own or their students' immediate use within the teaching context. No other rights are granted without permission in writing from the publishers or under licence from the Copyright Licensing Agency Limited. Further details of such licences (for reprographic reproduction) may be obtained from the Copyright Licensing Agency Limited, of 90 Tottenham Court Road, London W1T 4LP.

Copy by any other means or for any other purpose is strictly prohibited without prior written consent from the copyright holders. Application for such permission should be addressed to the publishers.

Any person who commits any unauthorised act in relation to this publication may be liable to criminal prosecution and civil claims for damages.

Published in 2002 by:
Nelson Thornes Ltd
Delta Place
27 Bath Road
CHELTENHAM
GL53 7TH
United Kingdom

02 03 04 05 06 / 10 9 8 7 6 5 4 3 2 1

A catalogue record for this book is available from the British Library

ISBN 0 7487 6938 2

Illustrations by Tech-Set Ltd and Barking Dog Art

Page make-up by Tech-Set Ltd

Printed in Great Britain by Ashford Colour Press

Contents

	Introduction	5
	Record sheets	10
	Activities by key objective	
Numbers and the number system	Use symbols correctly, including less than (<), greater than (>), equals (=)	12
Rounding	Round any positive integer less than 1 000 to the nearest 10 or 100	14
Fractions	Recognise simple fractions that are several parts of a whole, and mixed numbers; recognise the equivalence of simple fractions	16
Calculating mentally	Use known number facts and place value to add or subtract mentally, including any pair of 2-digit whole numbers	18
Paper and pencil procedures	Carry out column addition and subtraction of two integers less than 1 000, and column addition of more than two such integers	22
Understanding division	Find remainders after division	24
Recalling multiplication facts	Know by heart facts for the 2, 3, 4, 5 and 10 multiplication tables	26
Recalling division facts	Derive quickly division facts corresponding to the 2, 3, 4, 5 and 10 multiplication tables	28
Using operations	Choose and use appropriate number operations and ways of calculating (mental, mental with jottings, pencil and paper) to solve problems	30
Measuring units	Know and use the relationships between familiar units of length, mass and capacity	32
Classifying polygons	Classify polygons, using criteria such as number of right angles, whether or not they are regular, symmetry properties	34
	Resource sheets	36
	Written assessment tests	71
	Mental mathematics tests	81
	Answers	89

Introduction

The *Assess and Review Year 4/P5* programme

Nelson Thornes Assess and Review Year 4/P5 is a mathematics assessment programme designed for use with children in Year 4 and meeting the assessment requirements of the *Framework for Teaching Mathematics* and the National Curricula for England and Wales. It offers a variety of assessment activities for each of the key objectives for Year 4 together with photocopiable resources and teaching notes. The programme can also be used in conjunction with the *National Guidelines for Scotland 5–14*.

The *Assess and Review Year 4/P5* book

This book provides teachers with a complete resource for assessing children's learning particularly in the medium term. A variety of assessment activities for individuals, pairs and groups are offered for each key objective. These have been carefully chosen for use within a medium term assessment lesson and to allow for as much teacher observation and questioning intervention as possible. For each activity, there are suggestions for probing questions, checkpoints, and possible weaknesses to look out for together with ideas for further remediating experiences. Photocopiable resource sheets for use with activities are provided towards the back of the book. Two written tests, two mental tests and individual and class record sheets are also provided.

The *Assess and Review Year 4/P5* philosophy

Children learn in a variety of ways. To make valid assessments of children's mathematical understanding, they need to be observed engaged in different types of activity such as written, mental and oral activities and games such as those provided in the *Assess and Review Year 4/P5* programme.

Observing children working together at an activity, either in pairs or a group, and listening to their dialogue can give an insight into children's thinking. It is also an efficient means of assessment, making the best use of teacher time. *Assess and Review Year 4/P5* provides a combination of individual, paired and group activities.

Well thought-out, probing questions from the teacher to the child, such as those provided with each activity in *Assess and Review Year 4/P5* are an essential element in assessing the level of children's understanding.

Teachers need to know what to look out for when assessing a child's understanding of a particular mathematical concept. *Assess and Review Year 4/P5* provides some pointers.

The National Curricula for England and Wales

The activities in this book support assessment for children at Key Stage 2 working within levels 3 to 4 of the National Curricula for England and Wales. In particular, they support assessment of all of the key objectives of the National Numeracy Framework for Year 4, namely:

- Use symbols correctly, including less than ($<$), greater than ($>$), equals ($=$)
- Round any positive integer less than 1 000 to the nearest 10 or 100
- Recognise simple fractions that are several parts of a whole, and mixed numbers; recognise the equivalence of simple fractions
- Use known number facts and place value to add or subtract mentally, including any pair of 2-digit whole numbers
- Carry out column addition and subtraction of two integers less than 1 000, and column addition of more than two such integers
- Find remainders after division
- Know by heart facts for the 2, 3, 4, 5 and 10 multiplication tables
- Derive quickly division facts corresponding to the 2, 3, 4, 5 and 10 multiplication tables
- Choose and use appropriate number operations and ways of calculating (mental, mental with jottings, pencil and paper) to solve problems
- Know and use the relationships between familiar units of length, mass and capacity
- Classify polygons, using criteria such as number of right angles, whether or not they are regular, symmetry properties

The National Curriculum for Wales

The National Curriculum for Wales

The activities in the book will support assessment of most of the teaching of the programmes of study.

This table shows programmes of study and activities that can be used to support their assessment.

Programmes of study	Page	Activity
Understanding number and place value	12	Number compare
	12	Number choice
	13	Make it true
	14	Make a guess
	14	A round hundred
	15	Round up, round down
	16	Simple fractions
	16	Fraction spin
	17	Fraction snap
Understanding number relationships and methods of calculation	18	Mental adding and subtracting
	19	Add or subtract multiples of ten or hundred
	19	Make a round hundred
	20	Tens, hundreds and thousands
	20	Hundreds and thousands
	21	Add and subtract 2-digit numbers
	22	Column addition
	22	Column subtraction
	23	Shopping bills
	23	3-digit add and subtract
	24	Keep the remainder
	24	Division compare
	25	Division problems
	26	2, 5 and 10 times tables
	26	3 and 4 multiplication tables
	27	Find the answer
	28	2, 5 and 10 division facts
	28	Function machines
	29	Division sentences
Solving numerical problems	21	All sorts of problems
	30	At the zoo
	30	Consecutive numbers
	31	Word problems in the library
	31	Measures word problems
Understanding and using properties of shape	34	Symmetry
	34	Patterns
	35	Shape properties pairs
Understanding and using measures	32	Comparing measures
	32	Measure it!
	33	Familiar units

The National Guidelines for Scotland 5–14

The National Guidelines for Scotland 5–14

The activities in the book will support assessment of most of the attainment targets and their strands.

This table shows strands and corresponding activities that can be used to support their assessment.

Strand	Page	Activity
Range and type of numbers	12	Number compare
	12	Number choice
	13	Make it true
	14	Make a guess
	14	A round hundred
	15	Round up, round down
Measures	32	Comparing measures
	32	Measure it!
	33	Familiar units
Add and subtract	18	Mental adding and subtracting
	19	Add or subtract multiples of ten or hundred
	19	Make a round hundred
	20	Tens, hundreds and thousands
	20	Hundreds and thousands
	21	Add and subtract 2-digit numbers
	22	Column addition
	22	Column subtraction
	23	Shopping bills
	23	3-digit add and subtract
Multiply and divide	24	Keep the remainder
	24	Division compare
	25	Division problems
	26	2, 5 and 10 times tables
	26	3 and 4 multiplication tables
	27	Find the answer
	28	2, 5 and 10 division facts
	28	Function machines
	29	Division sentences
Fractions, percentages and ratio	16	Simple fractions
	16	Fraction spin
	17	Fraction snap
Symmetry	34	Symmetry
	34	Patterns
	35	Shape properties pairs
Right angles	34	Symmetry
	34	Patterns
	35	Shape properties pairs
Problem-solving and enquiry	21	All sorts of problems
	30	At the zoo
	30	Consecutive numbers
	31	Word problems in the library
	31	Measures word problems

Using Assess and Review

Short- medium- and long-term assessment

This book supports short-, medium- and long-term assessment. Activities can be used for different assessment purposes.

Short-term assessment: Specific activities to assess a key objective can be chosen at any time and used for assessment purposes.

Medium-term assessment: During the half-termly assessment week the book can be used to find specific assessment activities which support the key objectives taught during that half term. The results of the tests should be used to inform planning for the next half term.

Long-term assessment: There are end-of-year tests included in the book, both mental tests to read out, with accompanying photocopiable sheets for the children to record their answers, and photocopiable written tests, each of which covers all the key objectives.

Use the assessment record charts on pages 10 and 11 to record the outcomes of your assessments.

Each lesson has sections on:

- **Probing questions:** these are the questions to ask of individuals and small groups to assess the depth of their knowledge and understanding.
- **Checkpoints:** these give specific assessment criteria for the learning objective for that activity. Ask yourself these questions: Can the children do this? Do they know and understand this?
- **Watch for:** these identify what to look for to identify possible misconceptions.

At the end of the set of activities for each key objective there is a table that lists all of the Watch for points and gives suggestions for remediation.

How to use the book

The book is structured as follows:

- activities to support each key objective
- pupil resource sheets containing resources and written activities
- end-of-year written and mental tests.

Planning

For short- and medium-term assessment decide on the key objectives to be assessed, based upon what has been taught during the previous half term. For each key objective taught, plan an assessment lesson. Choose some activities from the book so that one or two groups can be self-supporting in their work, and that you can work with another small group. Prepare resource sheets as necessary. Decide which groups of children will tackle which activity, taking into account the evidence from your existing assessment records. Make a list of the probing questions that you would like to use with your focus group, either as a group or as individuals from within that group. You may want to focus your attention upon those children for whom there is so far insufficient evidence of attainment in the relevant key objective.

Structure of the assessment lesson

Decide whether one of the activities that you have chosen could be used as an oral and mental starter. Explain to the children that they will be working on assessment activities and say which aspect of their learning you intend to assess during that lesson. During the plenary of the lesson return to the probing questions and use these with the whole group to assess a broader range of children's learning.

Towards the end of the school year use the mental tests and written tests to assess all of the children. Compare the results of these assessments with your records (see pages 10 and 11) and ensure that the receiving teacher is aware of any forward planning issues for individual children from the results of these assessments.

Resource requirements

In addition to the photocopiable resources provided in this book, you will need the following:
1–6 dice
blank dice
paper-clips
counters
scissors
glue

Links with Can Do Maths

Links with Can Do Maths: the electronic maths programme

Can Do Maths offers a set of three CD-ROMs for each year in Key Stage 2, providing a worthwhile complement to the *Assess and Review* programme. Each CD-ROM is 'stand alone' and addresses the key objectives within a particular *Numeracy Framework* strand. Between them, the CD-ROMs provide a variety of games, activities and printable resources to add to the range of activities provided in the books. A teacher's section within each CD-ROM contains teacher's notes on each activity, records of children's performances in particular activities and other materials.

Can Do Maths Year 4/P5 links are listed at the end of each section in this book so that it is easy to find the relevant activities. Choose a CD-ROM activity that has the same key objective as the activities selected from this book. This will help the children to focus upon the particular aspect to be assessed. Decide whether to ask children to work individually at the activities or whether they should work in pairs. The CD-ROM activities can be self-supporting, but if possible ask an adult to work with the children using the CD-ROM, so that the probing questions can be asked.

There is further guidance for using the CD-ROM activities in assessment and review lessons and at other times within the *Can Do Maths* teacher's notes.

For more information visit the *Can Do Maths* web site at www.nelsonthornes.com/candomaths or contact the customer services team on 01242 267280.

Class record sheet

Names

Key objectives: Year 4

- Use symbols correctly, including less than (<), greater than (>), equals (=)
- Round any positive integer less than 1 000 to the nearest 10 or 100
- Recognise simple fractions that are several parts of a whole, and mixed numbers; recognise the equivalence of simple fractions
- Use known number facts and place value to add or subtract mentally, including any pair of 2-digit whole numbers
- Carry out column addition and subtraction of two integers less than 1 000, and column addition of more than two such integers
- Find remainders after division
- Know by heart facts for the 2, 3, 4, 5 and 10 multiplication tables
- Derive quickly division facts corresponding to the 2, 3, 4, 5 and 10 multiplication tables
- Choose and use appropriate number operations and ways of calculating (mental, mental with jottings, pencil and paper) to solve problems
- Know and use the relationships between familiar units of length, mass and capacity
- Classify polygons, using criteria such as number of right angles, whether or not they are regular, symmetry properties

Tests

- Written assessment test 1
- Written assessment test 2
- Mental mathematics test 1
- Mental mathematics test 2

Assess and Review Year 4/P5 © Ann Montague-Smith, Nelson Thornes Ltd, 2002

Individual record sheet

Name ....

Key objectives: Year 4	Page	Activity	Comments
Use symbols correctly, including less than (<), greater than (>), equals (=)	12 12 13	Number compare Number choice Make it true	
Round any positive integer less than 1 000 to the nearest 10 or 100.	14 14 15	Make a guess A round hundred Round up, round down	
Recognise simple fractions that are several parts of a whole, and mixed numbers; recognise the equivalence of simple fractions	16 16 17	Simple fractions Fraction spin Fraction snap	
Use known number facts and place value to add or subtract mentally, including any pair of 2-digit whole numbers	18 19 19 20 20 21 21	Mental adding and subtracting Add or subtract multiples of ten or hundred Make a round hundred Tens, hundreds and thousands Hundreds and thousands Add and subtract 2-digit numbers All sorts of problems	
Carry out column addition and subtraction of two integers less than 1 000, and column addition of more than two such integers	22 22 23 23	Column addition Column subtraction Shopping bills 3-digit add and subtract	
Find remainders after division	24 24 25	Keep the remainder Division compare Division problems	
Know by heart facts for the 2, 3, 4, 5 and 10 multiplication tables	26 26 27	2, 5 and 10 times tables 3 and 4 multiplication tables Find the answer	
Derive quickly division facts corresponding to the 2, 3, 4, 5 and 10 multiplication tables	28 28 29	2, 5 and 10 division facts Function machines Division sentences	
Choose and use appropriate number operations and ways of calculating (mental, mental with jottings, pencil and paper) to solve problems	30 30 31 31	At the zoo Consecutive numbers Word problems in the library Measures word problems	
Know and use the relationships between familiar units of length, mass and capacity	32 32 33	Comparing measures Measure it! Familiar units	
Classify polygons, using criteria such as number of right angles, whether or not they are regular, symmetry properties	34 34 35	Symmetry Patterns Shape properties pairs	

Tests	Comments
Written assessment test 1	
Written assessment test 2	
Mental mathematics test 1	
Mental mathematics test 2	

Assess and Review Year 4/P5 © Ann Montague-Smith, Nelson Thornes Ltd, 2002

Numbers and the number system

Key objective

Use symbols correctly, including less than (<), greater than (>), equals (=)

Activity 1 Number compare

Learning objective

Use symbols correctly, including less than (<), greater than (>)

Organisation

Pairs

Resources

RS1 *Numeral cards* (four copies per pair, using numerals 0 to 9); flip chart and pen

Activity

Write on the flip chart the numerals 5, 2, 7 and 3. Ask the children to suggest some 4-digit numbers that can be made with these numerals and write their responses on the flip chart. Then ask, *Which is the smallest number you can make with these digits?* (2 357). *Which is the largest?* (7 532). Write on the flip chart: 2 357 ☐ 7 532. Ask, *Using the same numerals, which number might go between 2 357 and 7 532?* When the children have suggested some possible numbers, write one of them in the box and ask them how they should place the symbols < and > correctly. When they understand what to do, ask them to work in pairs. Explain that they should take turns to take four numeral cards from the shuffled pile and make the smallest and largest numbers and one in between, and write them down using less than and greater than symbols.

Probing questions

- *What could the missing symbol be?*
- *How did you work that out?*
- *If the numbers changed to ... what then?*

Checkpoints

- Can the child use the symbols < and > appropriately?
- Can the child compare numbers to identify which is greater/smaller?
- Does the child check digits for place value when comparing numbers?

- Does not distinguish between < and >
- Does not use place value to help to compare numbers

Activity 2 Number choice

Learning objective

Use symbols correctly, including less than (<), greater than (>), equals (=)

Organisation

Individuals

Resources

RS2 *Number choice*

Activity

Give each child a copy of RS2 *Number choice* and ask them to complete the sheet. Explain that there are some 4-digit numbers to choose from for each question. They should complete number sentences which use < and > with the appropriate numbers. The second part of the sheet contains some word problems, using greater than and less than statements. As they work ask individuals the probing questions.

Extension

Encourage the children to invent their own examples of the first type of number sentence on RS2, then swap with each other and answer the new questions.

Probing questions

- *What could the missing number be?*
- *How did you work that out?*
- *If the numbers changed to ... what then?*

Checkpoints

- Can the child compare numbers to identify which is greater/smaller?
- Does the child check digits for place value when comparing numbers?

- Does not distinguish between < and >
- Does not use place value to help to compare numbers

Activity 3 Make it true

Learning objective
Use symbols correctly, including less than (<), greater than (>), equals (=)

Organisation
Individuals

Resources
RS3 *Make it true*

Activity
Let each child have a copy of RS3 *Make it true*. Explain that the sheet lists two types of question. The first ones contain a series of numbers which the children must complete by inserting correctly the symbols <, > and = such as: 400 + 600 = 300 + 700 *or* 900 − 200 > 500 + 100. The second ones have a bank of numbers from which to choose. The children must write these in spaces where the symbols are already in place, such as: 500 + 800 < 2 000 − 350.

Extension
Encourage the children to invent their own examples of the first type of number sentence on RS3, then swap with each other and answer the new questions.

Probing questions
- *What could the missing symbol/number be?*
- *How did you work that out?*
- *If the numbers changed to ... what then?*

Checkpoints
- Can the child use the symbols <, > and = appropriately?
- Can the child compare numbers to identify which is greater/smaller?
- Does the child check digits for place value when comparing numbers?

- Does not distinguish between < and >
- Does not use place value to help to compare numbers

Watch for	Further experiences
Does not distinguish between < and >	Provide further experiences using numeral cards and symbol cards. Discuss what each symbol means.
Does not use place value to help to compare numbers	Encourage the child to look carefully at the value of each digit and to compare the two numbers digit by digit.

CD links
See also *Can Do Maths* Year 4/P5 CD-ROM 1

Rounding

Key objective

Round any positive integer less than 1 000 to the nearest 10 or 100

Activity 1 Make a guess

Learning objective

Round any positive integer less than 1 000 to the nearest 10

Organisation

Groups of four

Resources

About 200 counters in a box; a page of writing from a non-fiction book; about 180 sweets in a jar; sheets of dotty paper; about 250 pennies in a jar; about 120 crayons in a large box; about 150 interlocking cubes on a large tray

Activity

Give each child a sheet of paper and ask them to write three headings on it: Estimate, Count and Rounded to the nearest 10. Ask them to look at each item in the resources list and to record their estimate for each one on their sheet. When the estimates are complete they decide in their groups on how to count the objects other than one by one. For example, they might pile the pennies into tens or put the interlocking cubes into fives. They then complete the sheet, recording their count and rounding the numbers to the nearest 10.

Probing questions

- *I rounded a number to the nearest 10. The answer was 220. What could I have started with?*
- *How can you tell whether to round up or down?*
- *250 people attended the concert. This number was given to the nearest 10. What is the smallest number that attended? What is the largest number?*

Checkpoints

- Can the child round numbers to the nearest 10?

- Does not recognise when to round up or when to round down

Activity 2 A round hundred

Learning objective

Round any positive integer less than 1 000 to the nearest 100

Organisation

Individuals

Resources

RS4 *A round hundred*

Activity

Give each child a copy of RS4 *A round hundred*. Explain that the first part of the sheet asks them to round the given numbers to the nearest hundred. The second part asks them to suggest what the original number might have been before it was rounded to the nearest hundred.

Extension

Give the children some 4-digit numbers and ask them to round them to the nearest thousand.

Probing questions

- *I rounded a number to the nearest 100. The answer was 600. What could I have started with?*
- *How can you tell whether to round up or down?*
- *900 people attended the concert. This number was given to the nearest hundred. What is the smallest number that attended? What is the largest number?*

Checkpoints

- Can the child round numbers to the nearest 100?

- Does not recognise when to round up or when to round down

Activity 3 Round up, round down

Learning objective
Round any positive integer less than 1 000 to the nearest 10 or 100

Organisation
Pairs or groups of four

Resources
RS1 *Numeral cards* (four copies, using numerals 0 to 9); RS5 *Round up, round down*

Activity
Give each child a copy of RS5 *Round up, round down*. Explain that the aim of the game is to be the first player to reach exactly 1 000 without going over. The children take turns to choose two or three numeral cards and make a number with them. They then decide whether to round their number to the nearest 10 or 100. They keep a running total on their sheet. If their total goes over 1 000 they miss a turn, ignore the last score, then try again on their next turn.

Probing questions
- *I rounded a number to the nearest 10. The answer was 550. What could I have started with?*
- *How can you tell whether to round up or down?*
- *800 people attended the concert. This number was given to the nearest 100. What is the smallest number that attended? What is the largest number?*

Checkpoint
- Can the child round numbers to the nearest 10 or 100?

- Does not recognise when to round up or when to round down

Watch for	Further experiences
Does not recognise when to round up or when to round down	Check that the child knows the rounding rule, and knows what to do about a 5. Include rounding up and down in the oral and mental starters.

CD links
See also *Can Do Maths* Year 4/P5 CD-ROM 1

Fractions

Key objective

Recognise simple fractions that are several parts of a whole, and mixed numbers; recognise the equivalence of simple fractions

Activity 1 Simple fractions

Learning objective

Recognise simple fractions that are several parts of a whole; recognise the equivalence of simple fractions

Organisation

Individuals

Resources

RS6 *Simple fractions*; flip chart and pen

Activity

On the flip chart draw six counters and shade three of them. Ask, *What fraction is shaded?* Children may reply $\frac{3}{6}$ or $\frac{1}{2}$. Discuss which is the more usual way of writing this fraction. Then invite a child to write the fraction in words. Give each child a copy of RS6 *Simple fractions*. Explain that for each set of items on the sheet some of them are shaded. Ask the children to write the fraction shaded both in numerals and in words.

Probing questions

- *Tell me some fractions that are equivalent to $\frac{1}{2}$, $\frac{1}{3}$, $\frac{1}{4}$, $\frac{3}{4}$, $\frac{2}{3}$, ...*
- *Tell me some fractions that are greater than $\frac{1}{2}$. How do you know? Tell me some fractions that are greater than 1.*

Checkpoints

- Can the child identify simple fractions that are several parts of a whole, such as $\frac{2}{3}$ or $\frac{5}{8}$?
- Can the child identify equivalent simple fractions such as $\frac{1}{2}$, $\frac{1}{4}$ or $\frac{3}{4}$?

- Recognises unit fractions, such as $\frac{1}{2}$ and $\frac{1}{4}$, but does not recognise fractions such as $\frac{2}{4}$ being the same as $\frac{1}{2}$
- Where mixed numbers are included, fails to relate the whole number to the fraction

Activity 2 Fraction spin

Learning objective

Recognise simple fractions that are several parts of a whole, and mixed numbers; recognise the equivalence of simple fractions

Organisation

Pairs

Resources

RS7 *Fraction spin*; paper-clips

Activity

Let each child have a copy of RS7 *Fraction spin*. Explain that they take turns to spin a paper-clip twice on the number wheel, so that they have two numbers, such as 4 and 6. They make a fraction with their numbers then put the fraction into its simplest form, for example they change $\frac{4}{6}$ to $\frac{2}{3}$. They should also consider whether they can make two fractions with their numbers, such as $\frac{6}{4}$ which is the same as $1\frac{2}{4}$ or $1\frac{1}{2}$. After ten goes each, the winner is the child who has made the most fractions.

Probing questions

- *Tell me some fractions that are equivalent to $\frac{1}{2}$, $\frac{1}{3}$, $\frac{1}{4}$, $\frac{3}{4}$, $\frac{2}{3}$...*
- *Tell me which simple fraction is equivalent to $\frac{2}{4}$, $\frac{3}{6}$, $\frac{5}{10}$, $\frac{6}{8}$ ...*
- *Tell me some fractions that are greater than $\frac{1}{2}$. How do you know?*

Checkpoints

- Can the child identify simple fractions that are several parts of a whole, such as $\frac{2}{3}$ or $\frac{5}{8}$?
- Can the child identify equivalent simple fractions such as $\frac{1}{2}$, $\frac{1}{4}$ or $\frac{3}{4}$?
- Can the child identify mixed fractions such as $5\frac{1}{2}$?

- Recognises unit fractions, such as $\frac{1}{2}$ and $\frac{1}{4}$, but does not recognise fractions such as $\frac{2}{4}$ being the same as $\frac{1}{2}$

Activity 3 Fraction snap

Learning objective
Recognise simple fractions that are several parts of a whole; recognise the equivalence of simple fractions

Organisation
Pairs

Resources
RS8 *Fraction snap*; scissors

Activity
Give each pair a copy of RS8 *Fraction snap* cards and ask them to cut out the two sets of cards. In pairs they shuffle each set of cards and place them face down in a pile. They take turns to turn over the top card in each set. If the cards show equivalent or matching fractions, the first one to say 'Snap' takes the turned-up cards. The winner is the child who takes most of the cards.

Extension
The children could play Pairs with one set of the cards. This game relies on memory as well as an understanding of equivalent fractions.

Probing questions
- ***Tell me some fractions that are equivalent to $\frac{1}{2}$, $\frac{1}{3}$, $\frac{1}{4}$, $\frac{3}{4}$, $\frac{2}{3}$ ...***
- ***Tell me which simple fraction is equivalent to $\frac{2}{4}$, $\frac{3}{6}$, $\frac{5}{10}$, $\frac{6}{8}$ ...***
- ***Tell me some fractions that are greater than $\frac{1}{2}$. How do you know?***

Checkpoints
- Can the child identify simple fractions that are several parts of a whole, such as $\frac{2}{3}$ or $\frac{5}{8}$?
- Can the child identify equivalent simple fractions such as $\frac{1}{2}$, $\frac{1}{4}$ or $\frac{3}{4}$?

- Recognises unit fractions, such as $\frac{1}{2}$ and $\frac{1}{4}$, but does not recognise fractions such as $\frac{2}{4}$ being the same as $\frac{1}{2}$

Watch for	Further experiences
Recognises unit fractions, such as $\frac{1}{2}$ and $\frac{1}{4}$, but does not recognise fractions such as $\frac{2}{4}$ being the same as $\frac{1}{2}$	Provide further practical experience of working with objects and expressing how many have been ringed as a fraction, such as 5 out of 8 buttons is $\frac{5}{8}$.
Where mixed numbers are included, fails to relate the whole number to the fraction	Provide further experiences of considering whole numbers and fractions in a practical context, such as portions of bars of chocolate, for example for 3 whole bars and 5 out of 8 squares of chocolate, the fraction would be $3\frac{5}{8}$.

CD links
See also *Can Do Maths* Year 4/P5 CD-ROM 1

Calculating mentally

Key objective

Use known number facts and place value to add or subtract mentally, including any pair of 2-digit whole numbers

Activity 1 Mental adding and subtracting

Learning objective
Use known number facts and place value to add or subtract mentally, including any pair of 2-digit whole numbers

Organisation
Whole class, working individually

Resources
RS9 *Mental adding and subtracting*; coloured pencils

Activity
RS9 *Mental adding and subtracting* contains four different sets of questions for oral and mental starters, as follows:

1. adding and subtracting multiples of tens and hundreds
2. adding and subtracting 2- and 3-digit numbers to multiples of tens or hundreds
3. adding and subtracting a single-digit number from 3- or 4-digit numbers; finding differences between 'near' numbers
4. adding and subtracting any pair of 2-digit numbers.

Give each child a sheet of paper and ask them to write their name on the top and the numbers 1 to 15 down the side. Explain that you will ask them some oral questions and they should write down the answers. Some of the questions contain missing numbers. Read these as, *What should I add/subtract to ... to make ...?* At the end, mark the work together. The children can use coloured pencils to correct their work. Ask individuals the probing questions.

Probing questions
- *What strategy did you use to work out the answer?*
- *Could you use a different method?*
- *How could you check that your answer is correct?*

Checkpoints
- Can the child respond correctly to addition and subtraction questions, using known number facts, and place value?

- Does not have an efficient strategy for specific addition or subtraction questions

Activity 2: Add or subtract multiples of ten or hundred

Learning objective

Use known number facts and place value to add or subtract mentally, including any pair of 2-digit whole numbers.

Organisation

Individuals

Resources

RS10 *Add or subtract multiples of ten or hundred*; flip chart and pen

Activity

Write on the flip chart 40 + ☐ = 120. Ask *How could we work this out?* Invite the children to offer their solutions and methods. Now write ☐ − 40 = 70 and repeat the question. Repeat this for examples for crossing 1 000, such as 300 + 800; 900 + ☐ = 1 200; ☐ − 500 = 800. Give each child a copy of RS10 *Add or subtract multiples of ten or hundred* and explain that it contains examples of all of these types of question plus some word problems. Ask the children to work individually, and to write their answers on the sheet. Target individuals with the probing questions to test their understanding.

Probing questions

- *What strategy did you use to work out the answer?*
- *Could you use a different method?*
- *How could you check that your answer is correct?*

Checkpoints

- Can the child respond correctly to addition and subtraction questions, using known number facts, and place value?

- Does not have an efficient strategy for specific addition or subtraction questions

Activity 3: Make a round hundred

Learning objective

Use known number facts and place value to add or subtract mentally, including any pair of 2-digit whole numbers

Organisation

Pairs

Resources

RS11 *Make a round hundred*; counters in two colours; a timer

Activity

Give each pair a copy of RS11 *Make a round hundred*. Explain that with their counters the children take turns to cover two numbers which make a round hundred, such as 731 and 69. The children check each other's choices and can challenge if they think that an error has been made. They should give themselves 15 seconds to find a pair of numbers. If they fail within the given time, play passes to their partner.

Probing questions

- *What strategy did you use to work out the answer?*
- *Could you use a different method?*
- *How could you check that your answer is correct?*

Checkpoints

- Can the child respond correctly to addition and subtraction questions, using known number facts, and place value?

- Does not have an efficient strategy for specific addition or subtraction questions

Calculating mentally (cont.)

Activity 4 Tens, hundreds and thousands

Learning objective

Use known number facts and place value to add or subtract mentally, including any pair of 2-digit whole numbers

Organisation

Individuals

Resources

RS12 *Tens, hundreds and thousands*

Activity

Hand out to each child a copy of RS12 *Tens, hundreds and thousands* and explain that it contains some addition and subtraction statements, all of which involve tens, hundreds or thousands, plus word problems to solve. Ask the children to work individually, and to write their answers on the sheet. Ask the probing questions as they work.

Probing questions

- *What strategy did you use to work out the answer?*
- *Could you use a different method?*
- *How could you check that your answer is correct?*

Checkpoints

- Can the child respond correctly to addition and subtraction questions, using known number facts, and place value?

- Does not have an efficient strategy for specific addition or subtraction questions

Activity 5 Hundreds and thousands

Learning objective

Use known number facts and place value to add or subtract mentally, including any pair of 2-digit whole numbers

Organisation

Individuals

Resources

RS13 *Hundreds and thousands*

Activity

Let each child have a copy of RS13 *Hundreds and thousands* and explain that the statements all involve adding or subtracting single digits to hundreds or thousands, or involve subtracting near numbers. Ask the children to work individually to find the answers. There are also some word problems for the children to solve. Target individuals with the probing questions.

Probing questions

- *What strategy did you use to work out the answer?*
- *Could you use a different method?*
- *How could you check that your answer is correct?*

Checkpoints

- Can the child respond correctly to addition and subtraction questions, using known number facts, and place value?

- Does not have an efficient strategy for specific addition or subtraction questions

Activity 6 Add and subtract 2-digit numbers

Learning objective

Use known number facts and place value to add or subtract mentally, including any pair of 2-digit whole numbers

Organisation

Pairs

Resources

RS14 *Add and subtract 2-digit numbers*; paper-clips; scissors

Activity

Divide the children into pairs and give each pair a copy of RS14 *Add and subtract 2-digit numbers*. The children cut out the number cards, shuffle them and place them face down in a pile. They take turns to draw two cards, then spin the paper-clip on the operations wheel to determine whether to add or find the difference between the numbers. The child who draws the cards works out the answer and writes it down. Their partner checks the answer using a different calculation. For example, for 45 + 37 the partner could check by working out 82 − 45.

Probing questions

- *What strategy did you use to work out the answer?*
- *Could you use a different method?*
- *How could you check that your answer is correct?*

Checkpoints

- Can the child respond correctly to addition and subtraction questions, using known number facts, and place value?

- Does not have an efficient strategy for specific addition or subtraction questions

Activity 7 All sorts of problems

Learning objective

Use known number facts and place value to add or subtract mentally, including any pair of 2-digit whole numbers

Organisation

Individuals

Resources

RS15 *All sorts of problems*

Activity

Give each child a copy of RS15 *All sorts of problems* and explain that the word problems on it involve using number facts and place value to add or subtract mentally. Ask the children to work individually to solve the problems, writing their answers on the sheet. As they work, ask probing questions to test their understanding.

Probing questions

- *What strategy did you use to work out the answer?*
- *Could you use a different method?*
- *How could you check that your answer is correct?*

Checkpoints

- Can the child respond correctly to addition and subtraction questions, using known number facts, and place value?

- Does not have an efficient strategy for specific addition or subtraction questions

Watch for	Further experiences
Does not have an efficient strategy for specific addition or subtraction questions	Identify the strategy that the child is using, then teach one that is more efficient. Provide further opportunities to practise using this strategy.

CD links

See also *Can Do Maths* Year 4/P5 CD-ROM 1

Paper and pencil procedures

Key objective

Carry out column addition and subtraction of two integers less than 1 000, and column addition of more than two such integers

Activity 1 Column addition

Learning objective

Carry out column addition of two integers less than 1 000, and column addition of more than two such integers

Organisation

Individuals

Resources

RS16 *Column addition*

Activity

Let each child have a copy of RS16 *Column addition* and point out that the addition statements are written horizontally. Ask them to use the space on the sheet to re-write the sums vertically and to find the solutions using their chosen vertical method. You may want to suggest a method that they could use, such as:
- adding the most significant digits first
- compensation
- adding the least significant digits, preparing for carrying.

As they work, ask probing questions to test their understanding.

Probing questions

- *How did you carry out this column addition/subtraction?*
- *What did you have to think about as you completed this?*

Checkpoints

- Can the child complete column addition accurately?

- Does not align the digits correctly, so that place value position is ignored
- Does not carry the most significant figure

Activity 2 Column subtraction

Learning objective

Carry out column subtraction of two integers less than 1 000

Organisation

Individuals

Resources

RS17 *Column subtraction*

Activity

Give each child a copy of RS17 *Column subtraction* and point out that the subtraction statements are written horizontally. Ask them to use the space on the sheet to re-write the statements vertically and to find the solutions using their chosen vertical method. You may want to suggest a method that they could use, such as:
- complementary addition
- compensation
- decomposition.

As they work, target individuals with probing questions to test their understanding.

Probing questions

- *How did you carry out this column subtraction?*
- *What did you have to think about as you completed this?*

Checkpoints

- Can the child complete column subtraction accurately?

- Does not align the digits correctly, so that place value position is ignored
- Does not decompose the next digit where necessary

Activity 3 Shopping bills

Learning objective

Carry out column addition and subtraction of two integers less than 1 000, and column addition of more than two such integers

Organisation

Individuals

Resources

RS18 *Shopping bills*

Activity

Hand out a copy of RS18 *Shopping bills* to each child. Ask them to choose three items on the sheet and work out their change from £10. Remind them to use column addition and subtraction to work out totals and change, using the grid area on the sheet. As the children work, check that they align the decimal points under each other. Target individuals with probing questions to test their understanding.

Probing questions

- *How did you carry out this column addition/subtraction?*
- *What did you have to think about as you completed this?*

Checkpoints

- Can the child complete column addition accurately?
- Can the child complete column subtraction accurately?

- Does not align the digits correctly, so that place value position is ignored
- Does not carry the most significant figure
- Does not decompose the next digit where necessary

Activity 4 3-digit add and subtract

Learning objective

Carry out column addition and subtraction of two integers less than 1 000, and column addition of more than two such integers

Organisation

Pairs

Resources

RS19 *3-digit add and subtract*; RS1 *Numeral cards* (two copies per pair, using numerals 0 to 9)

Activity

Divide the children into pairs and let each pair have a copy of RS19 *3-digit add and subtract*. Explain that the aim of the activity is to score as close as possible to 1 000 without exceeding 1 000. Ask the children to shuffle the numeral cards and place them face down in a pile. They take turns to draw six cards, make two 3-digit numbers and decide whether to add or find the difference between the numbers. They keep a running total on RS19 so that each new answer is added to the previous total. Tell the children that they have ten goes each.

Probing questions

- *How did you carry out this column addition/subtraction?*
- *What did you have to think about as you completed this?*

Checkpoints

- Can the child complete column addition accurately?
- Can the child complete column subtraction accurately?

- Does not align the digits correctly, so that place value position is ignored
- Does not carry the most significant figure
- Does not decompose the next digit where necessary

Watch for	Further experiences
Does not align the digits correctly, so that place value position is ignored	Children could use squared paper for working. Discuss the meaning of each digit in the numbers, and their place value.
Does not carry the most significant figure	Discuss the meaning of the digits and which one needs to be carried and why.
Does not decompose the next digit where necessary	Work through some examples with the child and discuss what is happening when the digit is decomposed.

CD links

See also *Can Do Maths* Year 4/P5 CD-ROM 2

Understanding division

Key objective

Find remainders after division

Activity 1 Keep the remainder

Learning objective

Find remainders after division

Organisation

Pairs

Resources

RS20 *Keep the remainder*; paper-clips

Activity

With the children in pairs, give each pair a copy of RS20 *Keep the remainder* and a paper-clip. Ask them to take turns to spin the paper-clip on the number wheel to generate the divider. The first child divides the generated number into 50, states the remainder and subtracts the remainder from 50. This then becomes the starting number for the second child. For example, if the divider is 3: 50 ÷ 3 = 16 r 2; 50 − 2 = 48. On RS20 the children record 50 as the starting number and the remainder (2) in the points column. The difference, that is 48, is then written as the next starting number. The second child repeats the activity with the new starting number and they continue until they cannot divide any more. The winner is the child with the most points.

Probing questions

- *Do all divisions have remainders? Why not?*
- *Can you make up some questions that have a remainder of 1? How did you do that? Now make up some with a remainder of 2, 3, 4 …*
- *Can you make up some divisions with no remainders? How did you do that? Why is there no remainder?*

Checkpoints

- Can the child use their multiplication facts to derive division facts?
- Does the child understand and recognise remainders?

- Does not relate multiplication facts to division
- Does not recognise that there can be a remainder after division

Activity 2 Division compare

Learning objective

Find remainders after division

Organisation

Pairs

Resources

RS1 *Numeral cards* (four copies per pair, using numerals 0 to 9)

Activity

The children shuffle the cards and place them face down in a pile. They each take three cards and make a 2-digit number which they divide by their other number. For example, if they draw 2, 4 and 5, they could make 45 ÷ 2 = 22 r 1, or 25 ÷ 4 = 6 r 1. Explain that the object is to make the larger quotient (in the examples, 22 r 1 is larger than 6 r 1) and to score a point. Ask the children to record the card numbers, the division and the points that they score in a table like this:

Digits	Division	Points
2, 4, 5	45 ÷ 2 = 22 r1	1

Probing questions

- *Do all divisions have remainders? Why not?*
- *Can you make up some questions that have a remainder of 1? How did you do that? Now make up some with a remainder of 2, 3, 4 …*
- *Can you make up some divisions with no remainders? How did you do that? Why is there no remainder?*

Activity 2 continued

Checkpoints
- Can the child use their multiplication facts to derive division facts?
- Does the child understand and recognise remainders?

- Does not relate multiplication facts to division
- Does not recognise that there can be a remainder after division

Activity 3 Division problems

Learning objective
Find remainders after division

Organisation
Individuals

Resources
RS21 *Division problems*

Activity
Remind the children that they can use their multiplication table facts to help them work out division facts. Ask, *If there are 20 pencils to be shared equally amongst 3 pencil pots, how many pencils will each pot have? Will there be any pencils left over? How many will be left over?* Give each child a copy of RS21 *Division problems* and ask them to work out the answers to the problems, showing their working on the sheet. Point out that one of the problems involves rounding the answer. As the children work, target individuals with the probing questions.

Extension
The children could make up some division problems of their own which would involve rounding the answer either up or down.

Probing questions
- *If I divide 22 by 3 is there a remainder? How do you know?*
- *Can you make up some questions that have a remainder of 0? How did you do that? Now make up some with a remainder of 1, 2, 3, 4 …*

Checkpoints
- Can the child use their multiplication facts to derive division facts?
- Does the child understand and recognise remainders?

- Does not relate multiplication facts to division
- Does not recognise that there can be a remainder after division

Watch for	Further experiences
Does not relate multiplication facts to division	Provide experience of working with multiplication and division trios, such as: $5 \times 3 = 15$; $3 \times 5 = 15$; $15 \div 3 = 5$; $15 \div 5 = 3$
Does not recognise that there can be a remainder after division	Provide practical experiences of division, using apparatus, such as dividing 15 cubes by 2, 3, 4, 5 … Discuss which divisions have remainders, and link this to the relevant multiplication fact.

CD links
See also *Can Do Maths* Year 4/P5 CD-ROM 2

Recalling multiplication facts

Key objective

Know by heart facts for the 2, 3, 4, 5 and 10 multiplication tables

Activity 1 — 2, 5 and 10 times tables

Learning objective

Know by heart facts for the 2, 5 and 10 multiplication tables

Organisation

Pairs

Resources

RS1 *Numeral cards*; a blank dice marked 2, 2, 5, 5, 10, 10; flip chart and pen

Activity

On the flip chart write $9 \times 5 = \square$. Ask a child to fill in the answer. Repeat for other examples from the 2, 5, or 10 multiplication tables. Divide the children into pairs and give each pair the numeral cards from RS1. Ask them to shuffle the cards and place them face down in a pile. The children take turns to pick a numeral card and to roll the dice. They each write down the multiplication and the answer. For example, if they draw an 8 card and roll a 5, they would both write down $8 \times 5 = 40$. Let them continue for about ten minutes. Challenge the children to work as quickly and as accurately as they can and to complete as many different multiplications as they can in the given time.

Probing questions

- *What numbers could you multiply together to make 40?*
- *What is the product of 5 and 2? And 2 and 5? What do you notice? Why is that?*
- *What is the product of 5 and 4? And 10 and 4? What do you notice? Why is that?*

Checkpoints

- Can the child recall multiplication facts for the relevant tables?

- Goes through multiplication table before answering, so does not yet have rapid recall

Activity 2 — 3 and 4 multiplication tables

Learning objective

Know by heart facts for the 3 and 4 multiplication tables

Organisation

Pairs

Resources

RS22 *3 and 4 multiplication tables*; paper-clips; flip chart and pen

Activity

On the flip chart write $8 \times 3 = \square$. Invite a child to fill in the answer. Repeat for another example. Now write $\square \times 4 = 24$ and ask the children to decide what is missing. Ask them to explain how they worked out the answer. Divide the children into pairs and give each pair a copy of RS22 *3 and 4 multiplication tables*. Explain that it is a spinner game requiring them to write the 3 and 4 multiplication tables. Challenge the children to complete the work as quickly as possible, in about ten minutes.

Probing questions

- *The product is 24. What numbers could have been multiplied together?*
- *What is 3 multiplied by 4? What is 4 multiplied by 3? What do you notice about these multiplications? Can you explain this?*
- *How many multiplications do you know which give the answer of 12? 16? 20? 30?*

Checkpoints

- Can the child recall multiplication facts for the relevant tables?

- Goes through multiplication table before answering, so does not yet have rapid recall

Activity 3 Find the answer

Learning objective
Know by heart facts for the 2, 3, 4, 5 and 10 multiplication tables

Organisation
Pairs

Resources
RS23 Find the answer (also enlarged to A3 size); 30 counters in two colours; flip chart and pen

Activity
Pin the A3 copy of RS23 Find the answer to the flip chart. Explain that the numbers in the grid belong to the 2, 3, 4, 5 and 10 multiplication tables and that some of the numbers belong to more than one table. Tell them that the object of the game is to choose a number from the grid and to write a 2, 3, 4, 5 or 10 multiplication table fact. For example, circle 24 on the grid and ask the children to give you some facts about it such as 6×4, 8×3, 12×2. Write these facts in the space below the grid. Divide the children into pairs and give each pair a copy of RS23. Ask them to take turns to choose a number, cover it with a counter and write a fact about it. Their partner can score a point if they can also write a different fact. When all of the numbers in the grid have been covered, they total how many facts they have written. The winner is the child who has written the most.

Probing questions
- *The product is 30. What numbers could have been multiplied together?*
- *What is 5 multiplied by 4? What is 4 multiplied by 5? What do you notice about these multiplications? Can you explain this?*
- *How many multiplications do you know which give the answer of 18? 24? 40? 50?*

Checkpoints
- Can the child recall multiplication facts for the relevant tables?

- Goes through multiplication table before answering, so does not yet have rapid recall

Watch for	Further experiences
Goes through multiplication table before answering, so does not yet have rapid recall	Provide further opportunities to recall multiplication facts, and work with multiplication patterns, such as activities using a multiplication table, to develop rapid recall.

CD links
See also *Can Do Maths* Year 4/P5 CD-ROM 2

Recalling division facts

Key objective

Derive quickly division facts corresponding to the 2, 3, 4, 5 and 10 multiplication tables

Activity 1 — 2, 5 and 10 division facts

Learning objective

Derive quickly division facts corresponding to the 2, 5 and 10 multiplication tables

Organisation

Individuals

Resources

RS24 *2, 5 and 10 division facts*

Activity

Let each child have a copy of RS24 *2, 5 and 10 division facts*. Explain that their task is to complete division sentences and answer word problems involving division. Ask the children to complete the sheet individually, and as they work target individuals with probing questions.

Extension

Ask the children to find 2, 5 and 10 division facts for the number 200. Challenge them to explain how they worked these out.

Probing questions

- *How many multiplication and division facts can you make for the number 20? How did you work them out?*
- *How many multiplication and division facts can you make for the number 30? How did you work them out?*
- *How many multiplication and division facts can you make for the number 40? How did you work them out?*

Checkpoints

- Can the child use multiplication table facts to derive division facts?

- Does not relate multiplication facts to division

Activity 2 — Function machines

Learning objective

Derive quickly division facts corresponding to the 3 and 4 multiplication tables

Organisation

Individuals

Resources

RS25 *Function machines* (also enlarged to A3 size); flip chart and pen

Activity

Pin the enlargement of RS25 *Function machines* to the flip chart. Explain how the function machine works and where to write the answer. Go through the first example together and make sure that the children understand what to do. Give each child a copy of RS25 and ask them to work individually to complete the rest of the sheet. As they work target individuals with probing questions.

Extension

Challenge the children to find as many division statements as they can which include the number 48, 72, 144. Ask the children to explain how they worked them out.

Probing questions

- *How many multiplication and division facts can you make for the number 30? How did you work them out?*
- *How many multiplication and division facts can you make for the number 36? How did you work them out?*
- *How many multiplication and division facts can you make for the number 40? How did you work them out?*

Checkpoints

- Can the child use multiplication table facts to derive division facts?

- Does not relate multiplication facts to division

Activity 3 Division sentences

Learning objective
Derive quickly division facts corresponding to the 2, 3, 4, 5 and 10 multiplication tables

Organisation
Individuals

Resources
RS26 *Division sentences* (also enlarged to A3 size); 40 counters in two colours; flip chart and pen

Activity
Pin the A3 copy of RS26 *Division sentences* to the flip chart and explain that the numbers in the grid are all part of division statements. Tell the children that the object is to choose a number and write a division fact about it. Do an example together. Circle 8 on the grid and ask the children for some division facts about it, such as 8 ÷ 2 = 4 or 8 ÷ 4 = 2. Write these facts in the space below the grid. Give each child a copy of RS26 and ask them to write at least one division statement for each number in the grid.

Extension
Challenge the children to find as many different division facts as they can for these numbers: 40, 48, 60. They could work in pairs and check their answers with a calculator.

Probing questions
- *How many multiplication and division facts can you make for the number 36? How did you work them out?*
- *How many multiplication and division facts can you make for the number 40? How did you work them out?*
- *How many multiplication and division facts can you make for the number 50? How did you work them out?*

Checkpoints
- Can the child use multiplication table facts to derive division facts?

- Does not relate multiplication facts to division

Watch for
Does not relate multiplication facts to division

Further experiences
Give the children multiplication and division trios to work with, such as: 5 × 3 = 15; 3 × 5 = 15; 15 ÷ 3 = 5; 15 ÷ 5 = 3.

CD links
See also *Can Do Maths* Year 4/P5 CD-ROM 2

Using operations

Key objective

Choose and use appropriate number operations and ways of calculating (mental, mental with jottings, pencil and paper) to solve problems.

Activity 1 At the zoo

Learning objective

Choose and use appropriate number operations and ways of calculating (mental, mental with jottings, pencil and paper) to solve problems

Organisation

Pairs

Resources

RS27 *At the zoo*; optional counting materials (interlocking cubes, counters, number lines, hundred squares)

Activity

Give each pair a copy of RS27 *At the zoo* and read through the problem on the sheet together. Ensure that the children understand how to tackle the problem. As they work, discuss their thoughts with them. Encourage them to explain their reasoning and the mathematics they have chosen to solve the puzzle. If there is time, invite alternative solutions. Note those who use counting materials to help them as they may lack confidence to use their mathematical knowledge and understanding to solve problems.

Extension

If Mr Brown saw penguins, ducks, tigers, panthers and some snakes and counted 120 legs, how many animals could he have seen?

Probing questions

- *How did you decide which operation(s) you needed to use?*
- *How did you decide which operation to do first?*
- *Was there another way to solve this problem?*

Checkpoints

- Can the child use the operations +, −, × and ÷ appropriately?
- Does the child choose a sensible operation?

- Has difficulty recalling addition or subtraction facts
- Has difficulty recalling multiplication facts
- Has difficulty deriving division facts from known multiplication facts

Activity 2 Consecutive numbers

Learning objective

Choose and use appropriate number operations and ways of calculating (mental, mental with jottings, pencil and paper) to solve problems

Organisation

Pairs

Activity

Tell the children that you would like them to find three consecutive numbers which total 32. Ask them to work in pairs to solve the problem and to find a systematic way of recording their working. When they have completed this task, ask them to find other numbers up to 50 which can be made by adding three consecutive numbers. Ask the probing questions as they work.

Extension

Challenge the children to find numbers up to 100 that can be made by adding three consecutive numbers.

Probing questions

- *How did you decide which operation(s) you needed to use?*
- *How did you decide which operation to do first?*
- *Was there another way to solve this problem?*

Checkpoints

- Can the child use the operations + and − appropriately?
- Does the child choose a sensible operation?

- Has difficulty recalling addition or subtraction facts

Activity 3 Word problems in the library

Learning objective

Choose and use appropriate number operations and ways of calculating (mental, mental with jottings, pencil and paper) to solve problems

Organisation

Individuals

Resources

RS28 *Word problems in the library*

Activity

Give each child a copy of RS28 *Word problems in the library* and ask them to solve the problems. Explain that they will have to use their skills with place value, ordering numbers, fractions, addition, subtraction, multiplication and division. As they work individually, ask some of them the probing questions.

Probing questions

- *How did you decide which operation(s) you needed to use?*
- *How did you decide which operation to do first?*
- *Was there another way to solve this problem?*

Checkpoints

- Can the child use the operations $+$, $-$, $\times$ and $\div$ appropriately?
- Does the child choose a sensible operation?

- Has difficulty recalling addition or subtraction facts
- Has difficulty recalling multiplication facts
- Has difficulty deriving division facts from known multiplication facts

Activity 4 Measures word problems

Learning objective

Choose and use appropriate number operations and ways of calculating (mental, mental with jottings, pencil and paper) to solve problems

Organisation

Individuals

Resources

RS29 *Measures word problems*

Activity

Hand out a copy of RS29 *Measures word problems* to every child and tell them that they must use their knowledge of number facts to solve the problems on the sheet. Encourage them to work on their own, and as they do, target individuals with the probing questions.

Probing questions

- *How did you decide which operation(s) you needed to use?*
- *How did you decide which operation to do first?*
- *Was there another way to solve this problem?*

Checkpoints

- Can the child use the operations $+$, $-$, $\times$ and $\div$ appropriately?
- Does the child choose a sensible operation?

- Has difficulty recalling addition or subtraction facts
- Has difficulty recalling multiplication facts
- Has difficulty deriving division facts from known multiplication facts

Watch for	Further experiences
Has difficulty recalling addition or subtraction facts	Check which facts are proving difficult. Provide opportunities to learn these facts, such as hundred square games, use of number lines, and deriving unknown facts from known ones.
Has difficulty recalling multiplication facts	Check which facts are proving difficult. Provide opportunities to learn these facts, such as multiplication games, using doubles, and deriving from known facts unknown ones, such as 8×6 is the same as doubling 8×3.
Has difficulty deriving division facts from known multiplication facts	Check that multiplication facts are known. Provide opportunities to relate multiplication and division facts, such as $5 \times 4 = 20$ and $20 \div 4 = 5$.

CD links

See also *Can Do Maths* Year 4/P5 CD-ROM 3

Measuring units

Key objective

Know and use the relationships between familiar units of length, mass and capacity

Activity 1 Comparing measures

Learning objective

Know and use the relationships between familiar units of length, mass and capacity

Organisation

Individuals

Resources

RS30 *Comparing measures*

Activity

Give each child a copy of RS30 *Comparing measures*. Tell them that to answer the problems on the sheet they must use their knowledge of the relationships between different measures, for example that 1 000 metres is the same distance as 1 kilometre. As they work on their own, ask individuals the probing questions.

Probing questions

- *How did you decide how many of [this unit] there were?*
- *Can you tell me how millimetres/centimetres/ metres/kilometres relate to …?*
- *Can you tell me how grams and kilograms relate to each other?*
- *Can you tell me how millilitres and litres relate to each other?*
- *Which would you rather have, 720 g or $\frac{3}{4}$ kg of chocolate?*

Checkpoints

- Can the child relate grams and kilograms?
- Can the child relate millilitres and litres?
- Can the child relate millimetres and centimetres, centimetres and metres, and metres and kilometres?
- Can the child express measures using fractions?

- Does not recognise the relationship between measures of length
- Does not recognise the relationship between measures of weight
- Does not recognise the relationship between measures of capacity

Activity 2 Measure it!

Learning objective

Know and use the relationships between familiar units of length

Organisation

Individuals

Resources

RS31 *Measure it!*; a ruler marked in centimetres and millimetres; string

Activity

Let each child have a copy of RS31 *Measure it!* and tell them that they should measure the different illustrations on the sheet using string and a ruler. Explain that they should measure in both centimetres and millimetres, using fractions or decimals of centimetres where appropriate. Encourage the children to work on their own and while they do, ask the probing questions and ensure that they use their ruler correctly.

Extension

Challenge the children to suggest how they could work out how far a PE hoop would roll in one rotation. Then let them put their suggestion into practice. Ask them to justify the equipment they use and their unit of measure.

Activity 2 continued

Probing questions
- How did you decide how many of [this unit] there were?
- Can you tell me how millimetres/centimetres relate to ...?
- Which would you rather have, a pencil 6·5 cm long or one that is 35 mm long? Why?

Checkpoints
- Can the child relate millimetres and centimetres?
- Can the child express measures using fractions?
- Does the child use four rules to solve problems?

- Does not recognise the relationship between measures of length

Activity 3 Familiar units

Learning objective
Know and use the relationships between familiar units of length, mass and capacity

Organisation
Individuals

Resources
RS32 *Familiar units*

Activity
Give each child a copy of RS32 *Familiar units* and tell them that it contains word problems using both metric and imperial units. Explain that they must work out the answer to each problem and use the units asked for in the answer. Encourage them to work individually and ask the probing questions as they work.

Probing questions
- How did you decide how many of [this unit] there were?
- Can you tell me how millimetres/centimetres/ metres/kilometres relate to ...?
- Can you tell me how grams and kilograms relate to each other?
- Can you tell me how millilitres and litres relate to each other?
- Which would you rather have, 650 g or $\frac{3}{4}$ kg of chocolate? Why?

Checkpoints
- Can the child relate grams and kilograms?
- Can the child relate millilitres and litres?
- Can the child relate millimetres and centimetres, centimetres and metres, and metres and kilometres?
- Can the child express measures using fractions?
- Does the child use the four rules to solve problems?
- Can the child relate pints to litres?
- Can the child relate kilometres to miles?

- Does not recognise the relationship between measures of length
- Does not recognise the relationship between measures of weight
- Does not recognise the relationship between measures of capacity
- Is unable to choose the correct operation and use it appropriately

Watch for	Further experiences
Does not recognise the relationship between measures of length	Provide further practical experience of measuring with units of length and using equivalent units.
Does not recognise the relationship between measures of weight	Provide further practical experience of measuring with units of weight and using equivalent units.
Does not recognise the relationship between measures of capacity	Provide further practical experience of measuring with units of capacity and using equivalent units.
Is unable to choose the correct operation and use it appropriately	Provide further experience of answering word problems related to length. Ask the child to explain what mathematics is needed to solve the problem.

CD links
See also *Can Do Maths* Year 4/P5 CD-ROM 3

Classifying polygons

Key objective

Classify polygons, using criteria such as number of right angles, whether or not they are regular, symmetry properties

Activity 1 Symmetry

Learning objective

Classify polygons, using criteria such as number of right angles, whether or not they are regular, symmetry properties

Organisation

Individuals

Resources

RS33 *Symmetry*; mirrors

Activity

Let each child have a copy of RS33 *Symmetry* and explain that it is in two parts. The first part shows polygons. Ask them to sketch in the lines of symmetry in those shapes which are symmetrical and to tick all the right angles on these shapes. The second part shows half of a polygon and a mirror line for which they must complete the shape. Some children may need to use a mirror to complete the work. Make a note of those who do as they may need further practice in identifying lines of symmetry. As children work, target individuals with probing questions.

Extension

Ask the children to draw their own symmetrical, straight-sided shape and to show all of the lines of symmetry.

Probing questions

- *Is this a polygon? How do you know?*
- *Which of these shapes are regular? How do you know if a shape is regular?*
- *Which of these shapes have at least one line of symmetry?*

Checkpoints

- Can the child differentiate between polygons and non-polygons, and regular and irregular polygons?
- Does the child recognise symmetry in a plane shape?

- Does not recognise irregular polygons as belonging to the shape group
- Cannot find lines of symmetry in shapes

Activity 2 Patterns

Learning objective

Classify polygons, using criteria such as number of right angles, whether or not they are regular, symmetry properties

Organisation

Individuals

Resources

RS34 *Patterns*; scissors; glue; A4 paper

Activity

Hand out a copy of RS34 to each child and ask them to cut out the triangle shapes and place them on a sheet of paper to create a pattern. When they are satisfied with the pattern, they should glue it and then do the same with the L shapes. While they work ask the children questions about the angles of the triangles and the lengths of their sides. Target individuals with the probing questions.

Probing questions

- *Why do those triangles fit together?*
- *Which of these triangles are regular? How do you know if a shape is regular?*
- *Which of these triangles have at least one line of symmetry?*
- *Which triangles have right angles?*

| Activity 2 continued |

Checkpoints
- Can the child differentiate between regular and irregular triangles?
- Can the child sort shapes by their properties?
- Does the child recognise symmetry in a plane shape?
- Does the child know which triangles have right angles?
- Does the child know about the size of angles in equilateral triangles?

- Cannot find lines of symmetry in shapes
- Does not discriminate between equilateral and isosceles triangles

| Activity 3 **Shape properties pairs** |

Learning objective
Classify polygons, using criteria such as number of right angles, whether or not they are regular, symmetry properties

Organisation
Pairs

Resources
RS35 *Shape properties pairs*; scissors

Activity
Give each child a copy of RS35 *Shape properties pairs* and ask them to cut out the tiles. Explain that there are ten sets of paired tiles – a set with shapes on them and a set with descriptions of shapes. Ask the children to shuffle the tiles and spread them out, face down in an array. In pairs, the children take turns to turn over two tiles. If they choose a shape tile with its matching description, they keep the tiles; if not they turn them back over. When all the tiles have been collected, the winner is the child with the most matching pairs.

Probing questions
- *Is this a polygon? How do you know?*
- *Which of these shapes are regular? How do you know if a shape is regular?*
- *Which of these shapes have at least one line of symmetry?*
- *Which shapes have right angles?*

Checkpoints
- Can the child differentiate between polygons and non-polygons, and regular and irregular polygons?
- Can the child sort shapes by their properties?
- Does the child recognise symmetry in a plane shape?
- Does the child know which shapes have right angles?
- Does the child know about the size of angles in equilateral triangles?

- Does not recognise irregular polygons as belonging to the shape group, for example does not recognise an irregular hexagon
- Cannot find lines of symmetry in shapes
- Does not discriminate between equilateral and isosceles triangles

Watch for	Further experiences
Does not recognise irregular polygons as belonging to the shape group, for example does not recognise an irregular hexagon	Provide some regular and irregular polygon shape tiles and ask the child to sort them and to explain their sorting. Check that they recognise irregular shapes as being part of the specifically named set.
Cannot find lines of symmetry in shapes	Provide further mirror activities, in which half a shape is provided and the child asked to complete it. Also provide activities in which the child uses a mirror to find lines of symmetry in plane shapes.
Does not discriminate between equilateral and isosceles triangles	Use sets of triangle tiles and ask the child to sort these by type of triangle. Encourage them to describe each triangle by its angle and side length properties.

CD links
See also *Can Do Maths* Year 4/P5 CD ROM 3

Numeral cards

RS1

Photocopy onto card and cut out.

0	1
2	3
4	5
6	7
8	9	10

Assess and Review Year 4/P5 © Ann Montague-Smith, Nelson Thornes Ltd, 2002

Number choice

RS2

Name _____ Date _____

Use these numbers to complete the number sentences.

1395   2470   6547   9364   7384   6004

1	☐ < ☐	7	☐ > ☐
2	☐ < ☐	8	☐ > ☐
3	☐ < ☐	9	☐ > ☐
4	☐ < ☐	10	☐ > ☐
5	☐ < ☐	11	☐ > ☐
6	☐ < ☐	12	☐ > ☐

Now answer these questions.

13 Which is greater: 1560 or 1563? ☐

14 Is 3146 metres longer or shorter than 3246 metres? ☐

15 Which is heavier: 9646 kilograms or 9464 kilograms? ☐

16 Which is less: £10.36 or £10.63? ☐

17 Gosha walked 2463 metres. Sam walked 2436 metres.

   Who walked further? ☐

   How much further? ☐

18 John has 1430 game cards. Gupta has collected 1403 cards.

   Who has fewer cards? ☐

   How many fewer? ☐

Assess and Review Year 4/P5 © Ann Montague-Smith, Nelson Thornes Ltd, 2002

Make it true

RS3

Name _____ Date _____

Complete the number sentences using these symbols:

<   >   =

1. 400 + 600 ☐ 300 + 700
2. 900 − 200 ☐ 500 + 100
3. 450 − 300 ☐ 200 + 50
4. 940 − 800 ☐ 300 + 250
5. 320 + 450 ☐ 750 − 40
6. 870 − 170 ☐ 250 + 450
7. 620 + 340 ☐ 450 + 500
8. 460 − 150 ☐ 110 + 200
9. 750 − 250 ☐ 900 − 170
10. 240 + 350 ☐ 990 − 400

Use these numbers to complete the number sentences.

550   650   320   850   900   230   350

11. ☐ + ☐ < ☐ + ☐
12. ☐ + ☐ > ☐ − ☐
13. ☐ − ☐ = ☐ + ☐
14. ☐ − ☐ > ☐ − ☐
15. ☐ + ☐ < ☐ + ☐

A round hundred

RS4

Name _____ Date _____

Round these numbers to the nearest hundred.

1. 564 ☐
2. 931 ☐
3. 740 ☐
4. 804 ☐
5. 860 ☐

6. 550 ☐
7. 372 ☐
8. 458 ☐
9. 237 ☐
10. 149 ☐

What could these numbers have been before they were rounded to the nearest hundred?
Write three possible numbers for each one.

1. 500 ☐ ☐ ☐
2. 800 ☐ ☐ ☐
3. 1000 ☐ ☐ ☐
4. 200 ☐ ☐ ☐
5. 400 ☐ ☐ ☐
6. 700 ☐ ☐ ☐
7. 100 ☐ ☐ ☐
8. 300 ☐ ☐ ☐
9. 900 ☐ ☐ ☐
10. 600 ☐ ☐ ☐

Assess and Review Year 4/P5 © Ann Montague-Smith, Nelson Thornes Ltd, 2002

Round up, round down

RS5

Name .... Date ....

Play this game with a partner.

Shuffle your numeral cards.

Take turns to choose two or three cards.

Make a number with the cards and write it in the table below.

Decide whether to round the number to the nearest 10 or 100 and write this in the table.

Add your number to your previous number and write the total in the table.

The first one to reach 1000 wins.

If your total goes over 1000 miss that turn.

My number	Rounded to the nearest 10 or 100	Total

Simple fractions

RS6

Name .... Date ....

Write the fraction for the shaded part of each of these pictures in numbers and in words.

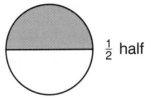

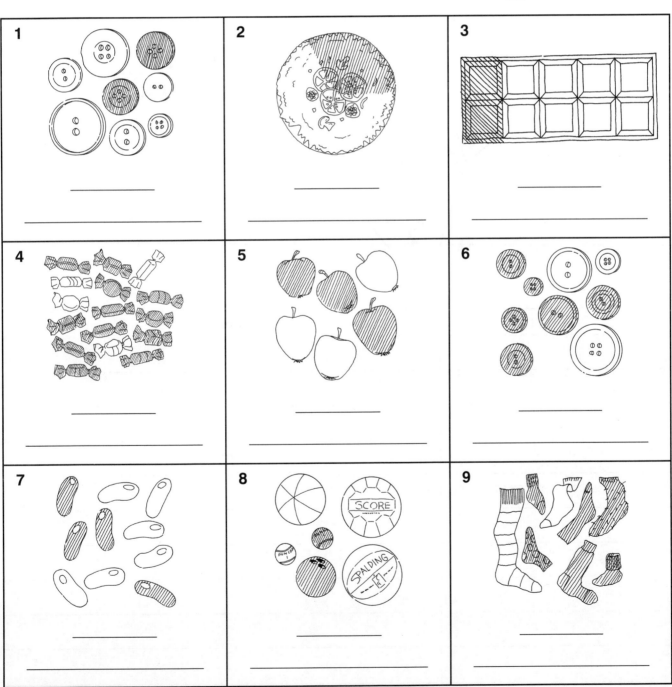

Fraction spin

RS7

Name -- **Date** --

Work with a partner.

Take turns to spin the paper-clip twice on the number wheel.

Use your numbers to make fractions.

Record your fractions in the space below.

After ten turns each, the winner is the one who has written the most fractions.

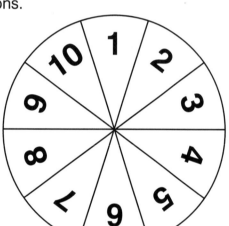

Numbers	Fractions
4 and 6	$\frac{4}{6} = \frac{2}{3}$ $\frac{6}{4} = 1\frac{1}{2}$

Numbers	Fractions

Assess and Review Year 4/P5 © Ann Montague-Smith, Nelson Thornes Ltd, 2002

Fraction snap

RS8

Enlarge the two sets of cards onto card and cut out.

$\frac{1}{2}$	$\frac{1}{3}$	$\frac{2}{3}$	$\frac{1}{4}$	$\frac{2}{4}$	$\frac{3}{4}$
$\frac{1}{5}$	$\frac{2}{5}$	$\frac{3}{5}$	$\frac{4}{5}$	$\frac{1}{6}$	$\frac{3}{6}$

$\frac{2}{6}$	$\frac{4}{6}$	$\frac{1}{8}$	$\frac{2}{8}$	$\frac{4}{8}$	$\frac{6}{8}$
$\frac{1}{10}$	$\frac{2}{10}$	$\frac{4}{10}$	$\frac{5}{10}$	$\frac{6}{10}$	$\frac{8}{10}$

Assess and Review Year 4/P5 © Ann Montague-Smith, Nelson Thornes Ltd, 2002

Mental adding and subtracting

RS9

Name _____ Date _____

A

1. 90 + 40 = ☐
2. 500 + 700 = ☐
3. 3200 + ☐ = 4000
4. 40 + 70 = ☐
5. ☐ − 500 = 900

6. 8400 + ☐ = 9000
7. ☐ − 30 = 60
8. 1200 − 600 = ☐
9. 130 − 50 = ☐
10. 7800 + ☐ = 8000

11. 1300 − 600 = ☐
12. 70 + ☐ = 150
13. ☐ − 20 = 90
14. 1500 − 900 = ☐
15. 7200 + ☐ = 8000

B

1. 51 + 30 = ☐
2. 93 − 40 = ☐
3. 80 + 28 = ☐
4. 70 + 56 = ☐
5. 71 + ☐ = 100

6. 581 − 30 = ☐
7. 540 + 23 = ☐
8. 9000 + 236 = ☐
9. 84 + ☐ = 100
10. 37 + ☐ = 100

11. 47 + 30 = ☐
12. 245 − 30 = ☐
13. 3000 + 268 = ☐
14. 327 + ☐ = 400
15. 562 + ☐ = 600

C

1. 539 + 3 = ☐
2. 8455 + 7 = ☐
3. 600 − 9 = ☐
4. 3000 − 2 = ☐
5. 805 − 8 = ☐

6. 5432 − 3 = ☐
7. 9002 − 8993 = ☐
8. 4006 − 3989 = ☐
9. 368 + ☐ = 371
10. ☐ + 6 = 1243

11. 6000 − 9 = ☐
12. ☐ − 3 = 4997
13. 6002 − 5899 = ☐
14. 3002 − 2984 = ☐
15. 1398 + 8 = ☐

D

1. 55 + 26 = ☐
2. 72 − 37 = ☐
3. 54 + 29 = ☐
4. 92 − 36 = ☐
5. 92 − ☐ = 57

6. ☐ + 29 = 83
7. ☐ − 25 = 56
8. 94 − 36 = ☐
9. 64 + 19 = ☐
10. 28 + 35 = ☐

11. 41 − 18 = ☐
12. 34 + 46 = ☐
13. 92 − 78 = ☐
14. 84 − 28 = ☐
15. 33 + 47 = ☐

Assess and Review Year 4/P5 © Ann Montague-Smith, Nelson Thornes Ltd, 2002

Add or subtract multiples of ten or hundred

RS10

Name _____ Date _____

Complete these number sentences.

1. 30 + 20 = ☐
2. 140 − 60 = ☐
3. 80 + ☐ = 130
4. ☐ − 60 = 70
5. 30 + ☐ = 110
6. 150 − 80 = ☐
7. 90 − 40 = ☐
8. 400 + 600 = ☐
9. 1300 − 500 = ☐
10. 200 + 800 = ☐

11. 700 + ☐ = 1400
12. ☐ − 700 = 900
13. 400 + 800 = ☐
14. 1500 − 900 = ☐
15. 3100 + ☐ = 4000
16. 8500 + ☐ = 9000
17. 7600 + ☐ = 8000
18. 1400 + ☐ = 2000
19. 9400 + ☐ = 10 000
20. 3200 + ☐ = 4000

Write the answers to these word problems.

21. What must be added to 6300 to make 7000? ☐

22. There were 30 pencils in one tub and 40 pencils in the other.
How many pencils were there altogether? ☐

23. What is the difference between 56 and 20? ☐

24. There are 3600 bricks. The builder needs 4000 bricks to build the wall.
How many more does he need? ☐

Assess and Review Year 4/P5 © Ann Montague-Smith, Nelson Thornes Ltd, 2002

Make a round hundred

RS11

Name .... Date ....

Work with a partner.

You will need a timer and counters in two colours.

Give yourselves 15 seconds for each turn.

Take turns to cover two numbers which make a round hundred,

for example 731 and 69 make 800.

The winner is the one who covers the most numbers.

634	28	41	238	7	47	248
19	581	36	387	94	129	719
66	53	62	106	71	493	264
972	75	859	81	325	52	13

Assess and Review Year 4/P5 © Ann Montague-Smith, Nelson Thornes Ltd, 2002

Tens, hundreds and thousands

RS12

Name _____ Date _____

Complete these number sentences.

1. 43 + 40 = ☐
2. 96 − 30 = ☐
3. 76 − 20 = ☐
4. 52 + ☐ = 92
5. ☐ + 20 = 62
6. ☐ − 10 = 85
7. 80 + 17 = ☐
8. 300 + 265 = ☐
9. 5000 + 592 = ☐
10. 520 + ☐ = 584

11. ☐ + 36 = 736
12. 940 + ☐ = 964
13. ☐ + 34 = 644
14. 570 + 21 = ☐
15. 158 + ☐ = 200
16. 387 + ☐ = 400
17. 921 + ☐ = 1000
18. 21 + ☐ = 100
19. 855 + ☐ = 900
20. 726 + ☐ = 800

Write the answers to these word problems.

21. What must be added to 147 to make 200? ☐

22. The farmer collects 122 eggs but 30 of these are cracked.
    How many whole eggs does he have? ☐

23. Dan counts how many sports cards he has collected. He counts 300 football cards and 146 basketball cards.
    How many cards does he have altogether? ☐

24. There are 30 children in the class. They each eat a biscuit from a pack. Now there are 18 biscuits left. How many biscuits were there to start with? ☐

Assess and Review Year 4/P5 © Ann Montague-Smith, Nelson Thornes Ltd, 2002

Hundreds and thousands

RS13

Name _____ Date _____

Complete these number sentences.

1. 618 + 4 = ☐
2. 317 + 7 = ☐
3. 9321 + 9 = ☐
4. ☐ + 4 = 293
5. ☐ + 9 = 1253
6. 3129 + ☐ = 3133
7. 700 − 6 = ☐
8. 300 − ☐ = 294
9. ☐ − 8 = 694
10. 5000 − 8 = ☐
11. 527 − 8 = ☐
12. 6435 − 7 = ☐
13. ☐ − 9 = 3214
14. 3146 − ☐ = 3138
15. 213 − ☐ = 205
16. 3004 − 2987 = ☐
17. 5006 − 4998 = ☐
18. 7004 − ☐ = 18
19. ☐ − 6987 = 15
20. 9007 − 18 = ☐

Write the answers to these word problems.

21. Three thousand, two hundred and ninety-eight people arrived on time for the pop concert. Seven people were late. How many people in total listened to the pop concert? ☐

22. There were 8000 bricks on the building site. A bricklayer took 7 bricks to finish a wall. How many bricks were left? ☐

23. The editor of a comic sent out 4006 questionnaires. Only 8 people sent back their answers. How many people did not answer? ☐

24. On Tuesday 4003 people looked at the new pop group's web site. On Wednesday 17 people fewer looked at the site. How many people looked at the site on Wednesday? ☐

Add and subtract 2-digit numbers

RS14

Cut out the cards. You will need some paper and a paper clip.

Work with a partner.

Take turns to spin a paper-clip on the + and − wheel and take two cards.

Write a number sentence for your cards.

Your partner will check your work by doing a number operation.

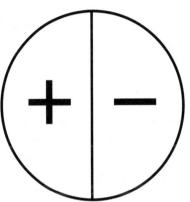

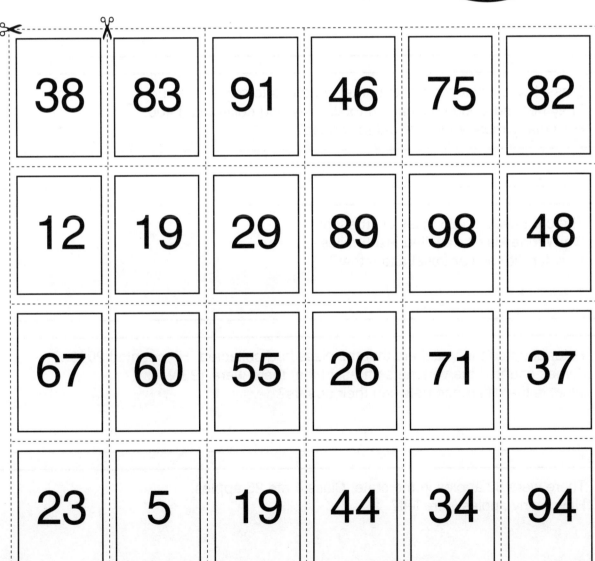

All sorts of problems

RS15

Name _____ Date _____

1. I think of a number then subtract 17.
   The answer is 35.
   What was my number?

2. Jane and Clare collected stamps from Christmas card envelopes.
   Jane collected 230 and Clare collected 65.
   How many did they collect altogether?

3. Class 4 was collecting supermarket vouchers to buy some sports equipment.
   They needed 4 000 vouchers in total. They had collected 3 400.
   How many more vouchers did they need?

4. The car travelled 428 miles on Tuesday.
   On Wednesday it travelled just 5 miles.
   How far did the car travel altogether?

5. Peter counted the vouchers that the class had collected. He counted 2006.
   James counted the vouchers and said that there were 1988.
   What is the difference between their counts?

6. There were 82 apples in the crate. Class 4 ate 25 apples.
   How many apples were left?

Assess and Review Year 4/P5 © Ann Montague-Smith, Nelson Thornes Ltd, 2002

Column addition

RS16

Name .... Date ....

Write these additions in the space below as column additions.

1. 438 + 36
2. 475 + 86
3. 463 + 78
4. £5.96 + 85p
5. £3.26 + £2.87
6. 219 + 84
7. 184 + 39
8. £1.59 + 74p
9. £2.95 + £2.95
10. £6.82 + £2.93

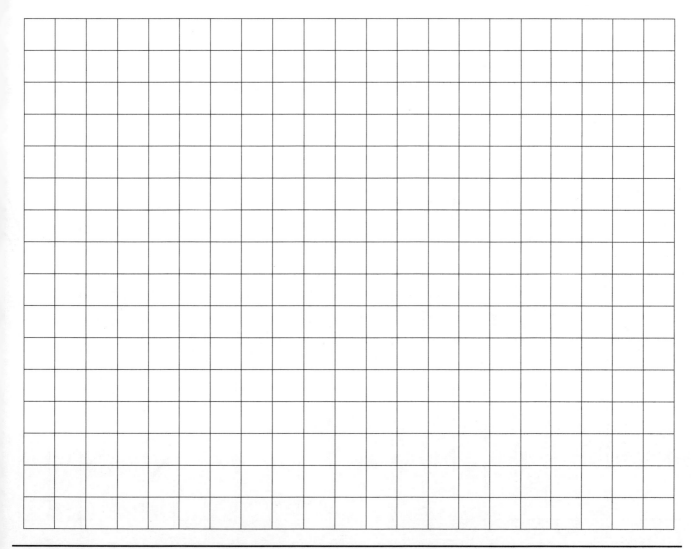

Assess and Review Year 4/P5 © Ann Montague-Smith, Nelson Thornes Ltd, 2002

Column subtraction

RS17

Name .... Date ....

Write these subtractions in the space below as column subtractions.

1. 296 − 37
2. 426 − 89
3. 545 − 68
4. 721 − 45
5. 328 − 49

6. £6.42 − 38p
7. £5.37 − 59p
8. £8.31 − 94p
9. £4.22 − 85p
10. £3.15 − 48p

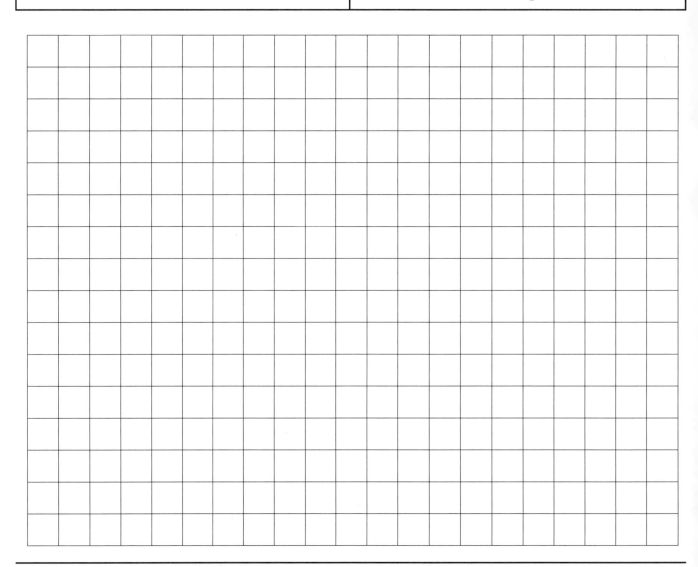

Shopping bills

RS18

Name ....   Date ....

You have £10 to spend.

Decide which three items you would like to buy.

Write a shopping bill and total it.

Work out your change from £10.

PACK OF TOFFEES
£1.25

BOX OF MINTS
£2.16

BAR OF CHOCOLATE
99p

BOX OF CHOCOLATES
£4.87

BARLEY SUGAR STICKS
85p

FRUIT DROPS
£1.29

MARSHMALLOWS
£1.08

SHERBET LEMONS
£1.57

I decided to buy

_____

_____

_____

Total

_____

My change from £10 is

_____

Assess and Review Year 4/P5 © Ann Montague-Smith, Nelson Thornes Ltd, 2002

3-digit add and subtract

RS19

| Name | Date |

Work with a partner.

Shuffle the numeral cards.

Take turns to take six cards.

Make two 3-digit numbers and write them down in the table below.

Decide whether to add or find the difference between the numbers.

Work out your calculation and write it in the table.

Put the answer in the running total column.

Do this several times, keeping a running total.

The object is to get as close as possible to 1000 in ten goes, without going over 1000.

Numbers	Sum or difference	Running total

Keep the remainder

RS20

Name .... **Date** ....

Work with a partner and decide who goes first.

Write your names in the table below.

First player, spin the paper-clip on the number wheel.

Divide 50 by the wheel number and write the division in the table.

Write the remainder as your points.

Subtract the remainder from 50.

Tell your partner that this is their starting number.

Repeat this, each time taking the remainder from the previous starting number to get the next.

Continue to play until there is nothing left.

The winner is the one with the most points.

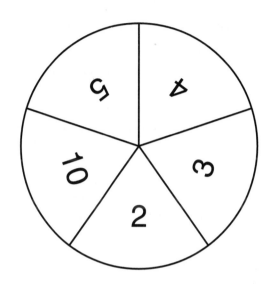

Name		Name	
Starting number and division	Points	Starting number and division	Points

Assess and Review Year 4/P5 © Ann Montague-Smith, Nelson Thornes Ltd, 2002

Division problems

RS21

Name .... Date ....

Write the answers to these problems.
Use the spaces to show your jottings.

1. John, Sammy, Dilip and Jo share equally a packet of 30 biscuits.
   How many do they have each?
   How many biscuits are left over?

2. There are 38 marbles in the box.
   How many each will 4 children have?

3. There are 43 oranges in a crate.
   How many can 5 children have each?
   How many are left?

4. Mrs Gur bought 24 eggs to make some omelettes.
   Each omelette needed 5 eggs.
   How many omelettes could she make?
   How many eggs did she have left?

5. A tube of choc chews has 36 sweets.
   If I shared these evenly among 10 children how many would be left for me?

6. There are 172 cars in the car park.
   The cars are parked in rows of 10.
   How many rows contain cars?

3 and 4 multiplication tables

RS22

Name _____ Date _____

In turn, spin a paper-clip on the number wheel.

Use the wheel number to complete a calculation from the 3 times table.

Repeat until you have eleven different facts.

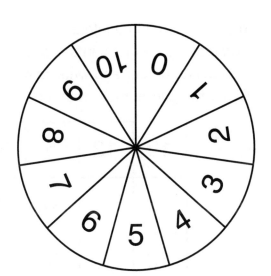

☐ × 3 =   ☐ × 3 =
☐ × 3 =   ☐ × 3 =
☐ × 3 =   ☐ × 3 =
☐ × 3 =   ☐ × 3 =
☐ × 3 =   ☐ × 3 =
☐ × 3 =

Now repeat this for the 4 times table.

☐ × 4 =   ☐ × 4 =
☐ × 4 =   ☐ × 4 =
☐ × 4 =   ☐ × 4 =
☐ × 4 =   ☐ × 4 =
☐ × 4 =   ☐ × 4 =
☐ × 4 =

Assess and Review Year 4/P5 © Ann Montague-Smith, Nelson Thornes Ltd, 2002

Find the answer

RS23

Name _____ Date _____

You will need 30 counters.
Some of the numbers in the grid are answers in the 2, 3, 4, 5 or 10 times tables.
Choose a number and write its multiplication fact (some have more than one fact).
Cover the grid number with a counter.

19	12	5	32	29	80	100	28	17	38
55	2	37	90	40	1	34	24	22	31
16	7	70	8	18	33	20	30	4	26
23	10	15	13	36	60	50	11	27	35

1 2 × facts

2 3 × facts

3 4 × facts

4 5 × facts

5 10 × facts

6 Which numbers are not covered by counters?

_____

7 How do you know that these numbers are not in the 2, 3, 4, 5 or 10 times tables?

_____

Assess and Review Year 4/P5 © Ann Montague-Smith, Nelson Thornes Ltd, 2002

2, 5 and 10 division facts

RS24

Name _____ Date _____

Fill in the answers.

1. $20 \div 5 = \square$
2. $36 \div 2 = \square$
3. $80 \div 10 = \square$
4. $45 \div 5 = \square$
5. $40 \div 2 = \square$

6. $120 \div 10 = \square$
7. $60 \div 5 = \square$
8. $50 \div 2 = \square$
9. $30 \div 10 = \square$
10. $25 \div 5 = \square$

Write in the missing numbers.

11. $30 \div \square = 3$
12. $40 \div \square = 8$
13. $\square \div 10 = 9$
14. $\square \div 2 = 6$
15. $\square \div 5 = 10$

16. $24 \div \square = 12$
17. $35 \div \square = 7$
18. $\square \div 10 = 10$
19. $\square \div 2 = 17$
20. $\square \div 5 = 9$

Write the answers to these problems.

21. What is thirty-five divided by five? $\square$

22. There are 20 biscuits in the tin. On how many plates can I put 10 biscuits? $\square$

23. How many pairs of socks can I make from 14 socks? $\square$

24. How many sets of five pencils can be made from fifty pencils? $\square$

Assess and Review Year 4/P5 © Ann Montague-Smith, Nelson Thornes Ltd, 2002

Function machines

RS25

Name .... Date ....

Write the numbers that come out of these function machines.

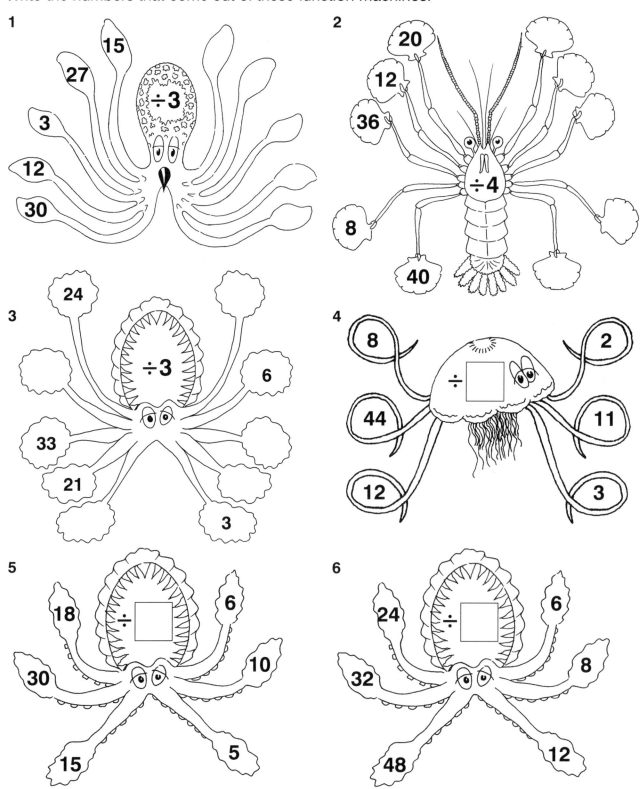

Division sentences

RS26

Name _____ Date _____

Each of the numbers in this grid can be used in a division sentence.

The sentences are dividing by 2, 3, 4, 5 or 10 and none of them have a remainder.

Write a division sentence for each number.

For example, for 14, $14 \div 2 = 7$.

Cross out the numbers when you have used them.

6	36	10	90	22	38
4	45	33	9	80	35
12	50	18	16	8	60
100	25	15	24	5	2

At the zoo

RS27

Name .... Date ....

Mr Brown is spending his lunchtime at the zoo.
He walks around, looking at the animals.
He sees some ostriches, elephants, zebras, monkeys, lions, and, of course, some humans.
He counts the number of legs that he sees and they total 100.
How many of each of the animals do you think he sees?

Record your work here.

Assess and Review Year 4/P5 © Ann Montague-Smith, Nelson Thornes Ltd, 2002

Word problems in the library

RS28

Name .... Date ....

Write the answers to these problems.
Show your working.

1   The Animal Encyclopaedia comes in ten volumes, each with 100 pages. How many pages are there altogether?

2   Someone has taken out the pages from a folder about plants and has muddled them up. The pages are numbered 312, 321, 123, 231, 213, 132. Please write them in order, starting with the lowest number.

3   The children in Class 4 love to read about sports, especially swimming.
There are 40 books about sports in the library. A quarter of these are about swimming. How many sports books are not about swimming?

4   Gill decided to count how many books there were on the transport shelf. She counted 16 about buses, 28 about fire engines, 31 about cars and 17 about ships. How many transport books did she count altogether?

Assess and Review Year 4/P5 © Ann Montague-Smith, Nelson Thornes Ltd, 2002

Measures word problems

RS29

Name _____ Date _____

Write the answers to these problems.
Show your working.

1 Sarah and Mark are going on holiday by car. They have to travel 354 miles to the seaside. They stop for a rest after 206 miles. How much further do they have to go?

2 Sarah and Mark left home at 7.30 am and arrived at the seaside at 4.15 pm. They stopped for a rest for 50 minutes. For how long were they travelling in the car?

3 On the beach were lots of pebbles, each weighing about 250 grams. Roughly how much do 10 pebbles weigh?

4 The family was thirsty so they shared a 2 litre bottle of pop. Dad drank 350 ml, Mum drank 250 ml, Sarah drank 220 ml and Mark 200 ml. How much was left in the bottle?

Assess and Review Year 4/P5 © Ann Montague-Smith, Nelson Thornes Ltd, 2002

Comparing measures

RS30

Name .... Date ....

Write the answers to these problems.
Show your working.

1. The milkman delivers 1500 ml of milk to Gerda's house every day. How many litres does the milkman deliver each week?

2. The children drink 250 ml of milk at school every day. In litres, how much milk does one child drink in a week?

3. Jodie walks from her home to see her grandparents. The distance is 2430 metres. How far is this in kilometers?

4. Sam's mother buys a 2 kilogram bag of potatoes and cooks 1·3 kilograms of the potatoes for supper. How many grams of potatoes are left?

Assess and Review Year 4/P5 © Ann Montague-Smith, Nelson Thornes Ltd, 2002

Measure it!

RS31

Name _____ Date _____

Measure these lines as accurately as you can.
Write their lengths in millimetres.
Do not forget to write the units.

1

2

3

4

Write the lengths of these lines in centimetres, using either a decimal point to show millimetres, such as 5·6 cm, or a fraction, such as $5\frac{3}{5}$ cm.

5

6

7

8

Assess and Review Year 4/P5 © Ann Montague-Smith, Nelson Thornes Ltd, 2002

Familiar units

RS32

Name _____ Date _____

Write the answers to these problems.
Show your working.

1 James walks ½ mile to school and ½ mile home again at the end of the day. About how many kilometres does he walk each week?

2 James' mother makes 2 pints of yogurt each week. About how many litres does she make in 4 weeks?

3 Every day James eats 2 oranges which weigh about 125 grams each. How long will a 2 kg bag of oranges last?

4 James' sister was 52 cm long when she was born. She now measures 1·26 metres. In metres, how much has she grown?

Symmetry

RS33

Name _____ Date _____

Look carefully at these shapes.

Draw in all the lines of symmetry.

Take care: one shape has no line of symmetry.

Then tick all the right angles on the shapes.

1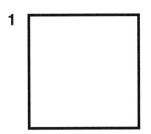

2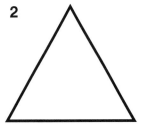

3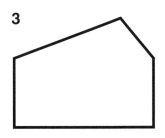

4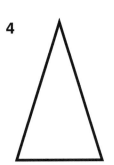

5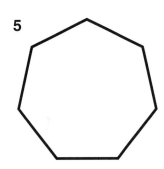

6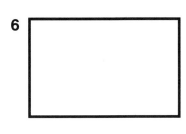

Only half of each shape has been drawn.

Use the mirror line to help you draw the reflection.

7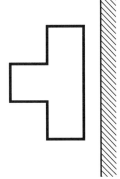

8

Assess and Review Year 4/P5 © Ann Montague-Smith, Nelson Thornes Ltd, 2002

Patterns

RS34

You will need scissors, glue and two sheets of paper.

Cut out the triangles and make a pattern with them.
Stick your pattern onto one sheet of paper.

Then cut out the L shapes and make a pattern with them.
Stick your pattern onto the other sheet of paper.

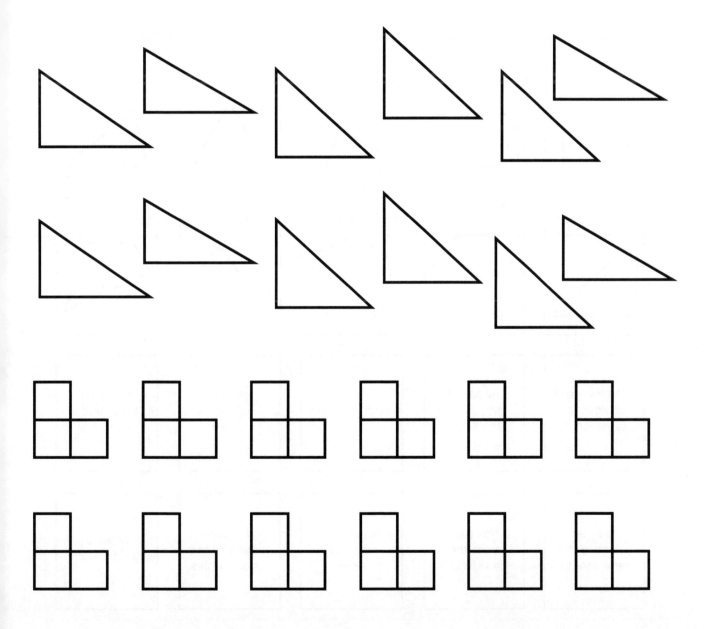

Shape properties pairs

RS35

Cut out all the tiles.

Work with a partner.

Shuffle the tiles and spread them out in a rectangular array.

Take turns to turn over two tiles.

If you have a shape tile and a matching description tile, keep them.

If not, turn them back over.

When all the tiles have been picked up, the winner has the most pairs of matching tiles.

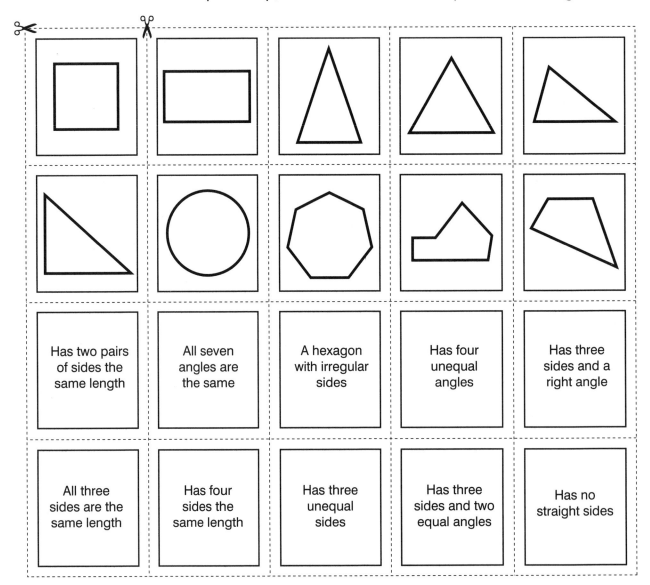

Assess and Review Year 4/P5 © Ann Montague-Smith, Nelson Thornes Ltd, 2002

Written assessment tests

Assessment tests

In this section there are two written tests and two mental mathematics tests. These tests can be used at any time after all of the key objectives for the year have been taught. They will be especially useful towards the end of the school year and will give evidence of achievement for the key objectives.

Written tests

There are two written tests to choose from. You may find it helpful, where children are sitting alongside each other, to use both tests, so that children will show their own work. Each test covers all of the key objectives. No time limit has been set for the test. Either allow the children to work until they have completed all of the questions, or decide upon a time limit, such as 45 minutes.

After you have given out the answer sheets and before the children start the test:

- make sure that they have a pencil and ruler with centimetres; explain that using calculators is not allowed
- explain that in most cases answers are to be written in an answer box
- explain that if they need to do any written working out they can do so anywhere other than in an answer box
- explain that in some cases there will be a larger box where they are actually asked to show their working; if they do not do this, they may not get any marks
- discourage the children from rubbing out; instead, they can put a line through an incorrect answer and put the second version alongside
- tell them how long they have to complete the test
- remind them that they must not talk during the test
- explain that if they find a question too difficult, they should move on to the next one and come back later if they have time.

During the test:

- informally monitor children's progress through the test and offer encouragement particularly to those experiencing any difficulties
- periodically tell the children how much time they have left.

If they finish the test early encourage them to go back and check their answers.

After the test is finished

Mark the answers. Where a child has made an error, refer back in this book to the relevant section for that key objective and use the probing questions and Watch for sections to help you to determine what further help the child will need.

Written test key objectives

The table below shows the question numbers from Written assessment Tests 1 and 2 that correspond to each Year 4 key objective. Each key objective has also been given a letter of the alphabet, which is displayed in the margin of the test paper next to the corresponding question.

Key objectives	Test 1	Test 2
A Use symbols correctly, including less than (<), greater than (>), equals (=)	2	1
B Round any positive integer less than 1 000 to the nearest 10 or 100	1	2
C Recognise simple fractions that are several parts of a whole, and mixed numbers; recognise the equivalence of simple fractions	3	3
D Use known number facts and place value to add or subtract mentally, including any pair of 2-digit whole numbers	4	4
E Carry out column addition and subtraction of two integers less than 1 000, and column addition of more than two such integers	5	5
F Find remainders after division	8	8
G Know by heart facts for the 2, 3, 4, 5 and 10 multiplication tables	6	6
H Derive quickly division facts corresponding to the 2, 3, 4, 5 and 10 multiplication tables	7	7
I Choose and use appropriate number operations and ways of calculating (mental, mental with jottings, pencil and paper) to solve problems	11	11
J Know and use the relationships between familiar units of length, mass and capacity	9	9
K Classify polygons, using criteria such as number of right angles, whether or not they are regular, symmetry properties	10	10

Written assessment

Test 1

Name _____ Date _____

Practice question

Write in <, > or = to finish this number sentence.

540 − 230 ▢ 95 + 200

1 Round these numbers to the nearest 10.

95 ▢   145 ▢   304 ▢   952 ▢

Round these numbers to the nearest 100.

463 ▢   949 ▢   350 ▢   545 ▢

2 Write in <, > or = to finish the number sentences.

35 + 49 ▢ 100   100 − 47 ▢ 45

500 + 400 ▢ 390 + 510   6 × 4 ▢ 8 × 3

3 Write the fraction for the shaded part.

a. 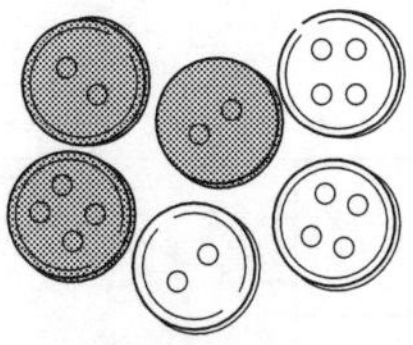 [buttons image] ▢   b. 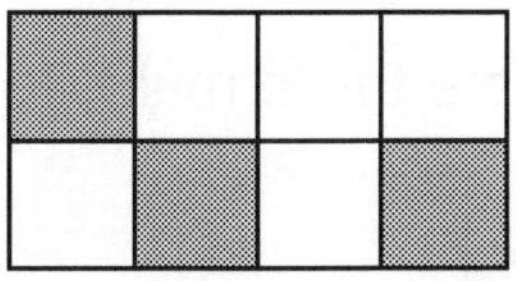 [rectangle grid image] ▢

c. 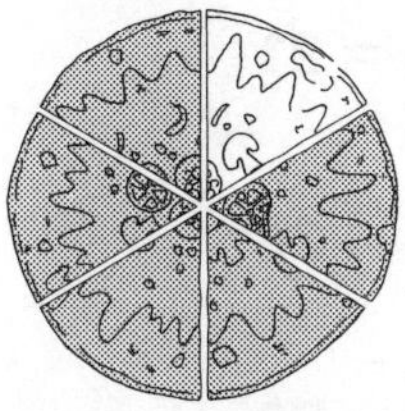 [pizza image] ▢   d. 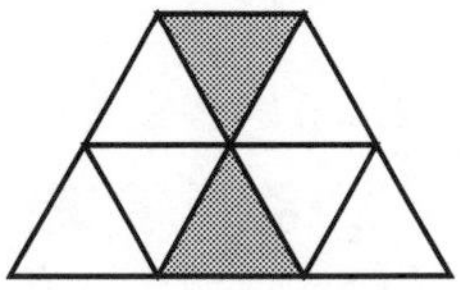 [triangles image] ▢

e. Circle the fractions that are equivalent to $\frac{1}{2}$.

$\frac{2}{3}$ $\frac{3}{6}$ $\frac{3}{8}$ $\frac{4}{8}$ $\frac{5}{10}$ $\frac{8}{10}$

Test 1

4 Write the missing numbers.

a. 60 + ☐ = 130

b. 300 + 900 = ☐

c. 943 − 30 = ☐

d. 510 + 57 = ☐

e. 8500 + ☐ = 9000

f. 6000 − 3 = ☐

g. 5006 − 4989 = ☐

h. 33 + 37 = ☐

i. ☐ − 40 = 90

j. ☐ − 500 = 800

k. 38 + 40 = ☐

l. 64 + ☐ = 100

m. 946 + 8 = ☐

n. 5432 − 8 = ☐

o. 54 − 37 = ☐

5 Clare bought a book for £4.39 and a pen for £3.78.
How much did she spend?
Write a vertical addition.

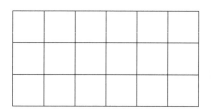

Clare had £9.36 in her pocket.
How much did she have left after she had bought the book and the pen?
Write a vertical subtraction.

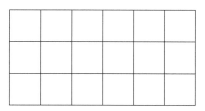

6 Complete these multiplications.

5 × 4 = ☐

8 × 2 = ☐

3 × ☐ = 30

5 × 5 = ☐

7 × 3 = ☐

9 × 2 = ☐

7 × ☐ = 21

☐ × 4 = 28

4 × ☐ = 20

9 × ☐ = 90

TOTAL

Assess and Review Year 4/P5 © Ann Montague-Smith, Nelson Thornes Ltd, 2002

Test 1

7 Use your multiplication tables to help you to fill in the missing numbers.

60 ÷ ☐ = 6   36 ÷ 4 = ☐

35 ÷ 5 = ☐   ☐ ÷ 3 = 8

40 ÷ 4 = ☐   45 ÷ ☐ = 9

☐ ÷ 3 = 9   60 ÷ 10 = ☐

☐ ÷ 2 = 9   14 ÷ ☐ = 7

8 Josh shared 24 biscuits among 5 plates. How many were left over?

_____

9 The map shows the distances, in kilometres, between three villages.

In metres, how much further is it from Bluewater to Downley than from Hampton to Bluewater? _____

Which weighs more, 650 g of cheese or 0·6 kg of cheese?

_____

David fills 5 cups from a 1 litre bottle of juice. He empties the bottle. How much juice, in millilitres, is there in one cup?

_____

Assess and Review Year 4/P5 © Ann Montague-Smith, Nelson Thornes Ltd, 2002

10 Join each shape to its properties label.

| Has 6 equal sides |
| Has 4 right angles and 4 equal sides |
| Is an irregular triangle |
| Has 5 angles, 2 are right angles, and 1 line of symmetry |
| Has 3 sides, 1 right angle and 1 line of symmetry |
| Opposite sides are the same length |
| Is curved |

11 There are 36 children in the class.

One third of them eat a banana at break.

Half of them eat an apple at break.

The rest of the children eat a chocolate bar.

How many children eat a chocolate bar?

Written assessment

Test 2

Name .... Date ....

Practice question

Round this number to the nearest 10.

85 ☐

1 Write in the missing symbol using <, > or =.

347 ☐ 482   946 ☐ 427   843 ☐ 834

654 ☐ 456   58 + 20 ☐ 42 + 36   95 − 43 ☐ 22 + 20

2 Round these numbers to the nearest 10.

96 ☐   37 ☐   23 ☐   48 ☐   52 ☐

Round these numbers to the nearest 100.

531 ☐   648 ☐   307 ☐   866 ☐   941 ☐

3 Shade in these fractions.

a.  $\frac{1}{2}$

b.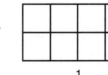
$\frac{1}{4}$

c.  $\frac{3}{8}$

d.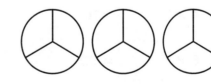
$2\frac{1}{3}$

e. Ring the fraction that is equivalent to $\frac{1}{3}$.

$\frac{1}{2}$ $\frac{2}{6}$ $\frac{3}{8}$ $\frac{5}{10}$

A 6

B 10

C 5

TOTAL

Test 2

4 Fill in the missing numbers.

a. 70 + ☐ = 120

b. ☐ + 400 = 1300

c. 46 + 30 = ☐

d. 520 + 46 = ☐

e. 2800 + ☐ = 3000

f. 4000 − 5 = ☐

g. 5003 − 4988 = ☐

h. 87 − 39 = ☐

i. ☐ − 40 = 80

j. 1300 − ☐ = 500

k. 95 − 60 = ☐

l. 37 + ☐ = 100

m. 467 + 8 = ☐

n. 5462 − 7 = ☐

o. 64 + 27 = ☐

5 The children in Class 4 saved 423 computer tokens.
In Class 5 they saved 278 tokens.
How many tokens had they saved in total?
Write a column addition.

Class 6 had saved 842 tokens.
They spent 453 tokens on some software.
How many tokens had they left?
Write a column subtraction.

6 Fill in the missing numbers.

8 × 2 = ☐

4 × ☐ = 16

6 × ☐ = 60

7 × 3 = ☐

☐ × 4 = 36

☐ × 3 = 15

2 × 5 = ☐

3 × ☐ = 6

4 × 5 = ☐

10 × 10 = ☐

Test 2

7 Fill in the missing numbers.

30 ÷ 5 = ☐   60 ÷ 10 = ☐

8 ÷ ☐ = 2   ☐ ÷ 3 = 3

20 ÷ 4 = ☐   35 ÷ ☐ = 7

80 ÷ 10 = ☐   ☐ ÷ 4 = 6

☐ ÷ 3 = 8   16 ÷ ☐ = 8

8 Petra had 26 cakes which she divided equally among 4 plates.
How many cakes were left over?

_____

9 How many pieces of string 90 cm long can be cut from a length 4·5 metres long?

_____

There were $2\frac{1}{2}$ litres of juice in the jug.
Dilip drank 500 ml.
How much juice was left?

_____

Jane bought $1\frac{1}{2}$ kg of potatoes.
Her mother cooked 800 g of potatoes for supper.
What was the weight of the remaining potatoes?

_____

Test 2

10 Answer the questions about this shape.

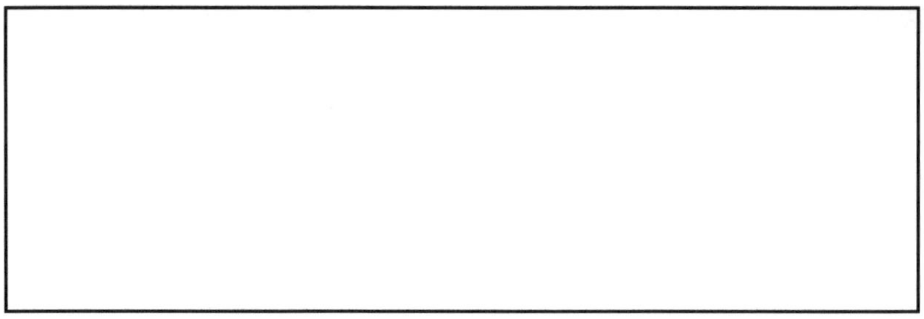

How many right angles are there?

_____

How many pairs of sides are the same length?

_____

What is the shape called?

_____

Now draw two lines of symmetry on the shape.

11 There were 8 cars and 6 motorbikes parked outside the school. How many wheels were there?

_____

Mental mathematics tests

Mental mathematics tests

There are two general mental mathematics tests. Each test contains twenty questions. Five seconds are allowed for answering each of the first ten questions; ten seconds for each of the second ten questions. Each test should take no longer than twenty minutes to administer. An answer sheet is provided for each test with aide-memoires for some of the questions.

Check that the children are sitting so that they can work individually. Provide each child with a pencil or pen and a copy of the answer sheet. Before the test begins, read out these instructions to the children:

- listen carefully to the instructions that I am going to give you; they will help you to complete the test
- check that you have an answer sheet and a pen or pencil *(pause)*
- you may not use an eraser, a calculator or any other mathematical equipment
- at the top of the paper write your name and the date *(pause)*
- there are twenty questions in the test
- work out the answers to the questions in your head before writing the answer
- there is an answer box for each question where you should write the answer to the questions and nothing else
- you may jot things down outside the answer box if it helps you
- if you write down a wrong answer, cross it out and write the new answer next to it
- try to answer as many questions as you can; if you cannot answer a question put a line in the box
- for some of the questions there is useful information on the sheet to help you, such as numbers used in the question
- I will read each question twice so you can hear it again
- there are two sets of questions; you will have five seconds to answer each question in the first set; this is five seconds: 1, 2, 3, 4, 5 *(count the seconds)*
- you will have ten seconds to answer each question in the second set
- you may not ask any questions once the test has started so if you have any questions ask them now *(pause long enough to allow any questions to be asked)*
- there will be a practice question to help you, then I will check that you understand what to do.

After the test is finished

Mark the answers. Where a child has made an error, refer back in this book to the relevant section for that key objective and use the probing questions and Watch for sections to help you to determine what further help the child will need.

Mental test key objectives

The table below shows the questions numbers from Mental mathematics Tests 1 and 2 that correspond to each Year 4 key objective.

Key objectives	Test 1	Test 2
A Use symbols correctly, including less than (<), greater than (>), equals (=)	2	1
B Round any positive integer less than 1 000 to the nearest 10 or 100	1	2
C Recognise simple fractions that are several parts of a whole, and mixed numbers; recognise the equivalence of simple fractions	19	18
D Use known number facts and place value to add or subtract mentally, including any pair of 2-digit whole numbers	3, 4, 9, 10	3, 4, 8, 9, 10
E Carry out column addition and subtraction of two integers less than 1 000, and column addition of more than two such integers		
F Find remainders after division	8	6
G Know by heart facts for the 2, 3, 4, 5 and 10 multiplication tables	5, 6	5
H Derive quickly division facts corresponding to the 2, 3, 4, 5 and 10 multiplication tables	7	7
I Choose and use appropriate number operations and ways of calculating (mental, mental with jottings, pencil and paper) to solve problems	13, 14, 15, 16, 17, 18, 20	13, 15, 16, 19, 20
J Know and use the relationships between familiar units of length, mass and capacity	11	11, 12
K Classify polygons, using criteria such as number of right angles, whether or not they are regular, symmetry properties	12	14, 17

Mental mathematics test 1

You will have five seconds to answer this practice question.

Point with your finger to where you will write the answer to the practice question.

Here is the question.

Round 78 to the nearest 10. *(repeat)*

Check that the children understand what to do. Now continue with the test.

You will have five seconds to work out each question and write the answer down. *(Read each question twice and then allow five seconds before reading the next question.)*

1   Round 44 to the nearest 10.

2   Look at the numbers on your sheet. Choose the symbol needed to complete the number sentence and write it in.

3   What is 54 subtract 28?

4   What is 35 add 27?

5   What is 7 multiplied by 3?

6   What is 8 multiplied by 4?

7   If 36 biscuits are shared among 4 plates, how many biscuits will there be on each plate?

8   Tim and Paul share 15 game cards equally between them. How many are left over?

9   What would you need to add to 63 to make 100?

10 What would you add to 4 300 to make 5 000?

You will have ten seconds to work out each question and write the answer down. *(Read each question twice and then allow ten seconds before reading the next question.)*

11 Look at the map on your sheet. If I walked from Monkton to Greenley, Greenley to Wixham, then Wixham to Monkton, how far would I walk in metres?

12 Look at the shapes on your sheet. The shape I am thinking of has a right angle and two sides of the same length. Put a tick by this shape.

13 Class 4 collected 320 tokens for sports equipment. They used 200 tokens to buy some football equipment. How many tokens were left?

14 To make enough biscuits for 2 people the recipe asks for 25 grams of flour. How much flour would be needed to make biscuits for 4 people?

15 Clare bought 4 tickets for the theatre at £8 each. How much change did she have from £40?

16 Class 4 need 5 000 tokens to buy some software. They have collected 4 100. How many more do they need to collect?

17 Cakes were packed in boxes of 4 at the factory. How many boxes were needed to pack 35 cakes?

18 The builder needed 6 004 bricks but there were only 5 987 bricks at the building site. How many more bricks did the builder need?

19 Look at the drawings on your sheet. Tick the one that shows one half shaded.

20 Anna has £5 pocket money to spend. She bought a pen for 75p and a book for £3. How much change did she have?

That is the end of the test.

Put down your pencil or pen and have your answer sheet ready to be collected.

Mental mathematics

Test 1

Name _____ **Date** _____

Practice question

| P | |

Time: five seconds for each question

| 1 | |

| 2 | 540 | | 630 | < > = |

| 3 | |

| 4 | |

| 5 | |

| 6 | |

| 7 | |

| 8 | |

| 9 | |

| 10 | |

TOTAL

Test 1

Time: ten seconds for each question

11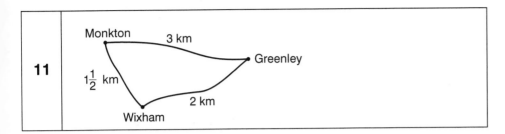

12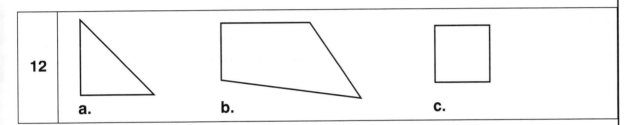
a.   b.   c.

13

14

15

16

17

18

19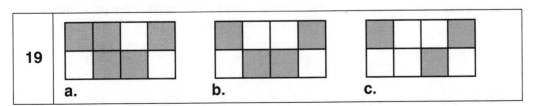
a.   b.   c.

20

TOTAL

Mental mathematics test 2

You will have five seconds to answer this practice question.

Point with your finger to where you will write the answer to the practice question.

Here is the question.

Read the number sentence on your sheet. Put a tick in the box if you think that the symbol is correct or a cross if it is not. *(repeat)*

Check that the children understand what to do.
Now continue with the test.

You will have five seconds to work out each question and write the answer down. *(Read each question twice and then allow five seconds before reading the next question.)*

1. Look at the number sentence on your sheet. Choose the correct symbol and write it into the box.

2. Round 968 to the nearest 10.

3. How many must be added to 2 400 to make 3 000?

4. What is the difference between 87 and 29?

5. Three children each had eight marbles. How many marbles were there in total?

6. If I share 18 pens among 4 children how many will be left over?

7. There are 32 cakes to be shared among 4 plates. How many cakes will there be on each plate?

8. How many must be added to 4 600 to make 5 000?

9. What must be added to 38 to make 100?

10. What is 93 subtract 46?

You will have ten seconds to work out each question and write the answer down. *(Read each question twice and then allow ten seconds before reading the next question.)*

11. Look at the measuring jug on your sheet. What fraction of a litre of juice is in the jug?

12. How many grams are there in $1\frac{1}{4}$ kilograms?

13. The distance from home to the seaside is 94 kilometres. When Jill has travelled 36 km how much further does she have to travel?

14. Look at the shape on your sheet. Draw in the line of symmetry.

15. There were 16 books on the top shelf of the bookcase, 18 on the middle shelf, and 12 on the bottom shelf. How many books were there in total on the bookcase?

16. James gets up every morning at five to seven and goes to bed at night at a quarter-past eight. How long is he out of bed each day?

17. How many sides has a pentagon?

18. Look at the drawing on your sheet. Write the fraction for the shaded part.

19. There are 30 children in Class 4. Ten children wore trainers to school. What fraction of the children did not wear trainers to school?

20. The factory needed to make 5 002 marbles. There were just 4 989 marbles made. How many more marbles were needed?

That is the end of the test.

Put down your pencil or pen and have your answer sheet ready to be collected.

Mental mathematics

Test 2

Name _____ Date _____

Practice question

| P | 532 > 941 | |

Time: five seconds for each question

| 1 | 432 | | 846 | < > = |

| 2 | |

| 3 | |

| 4 | |

| 5 | |

| 6 | |

| 7 | |

| 8 | |

| 9 | |

| 10 | |

TOTAL

Assess and Review Year 4/P5 © Ann Montague-Smith, Nelson Thornes Ltd, 2002

Test 2

Time: ten seconds for each question

11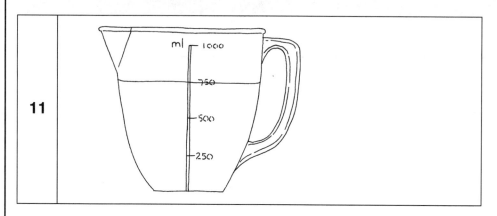

12

13

14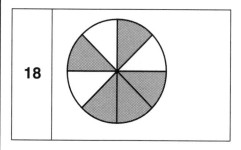

15

16

17

18

19

20

Answers

Resource sheets

RS2
1–12 answers will vary
13 1 563
14 shorter
15 9 646 kg
16 £10.36
17 Gosha; 27 metres
18 Gupta; 27

RS3
1 =
2 >
3 <
4 <
5 >
6 =
7 >
8 =
9 <
10 =
11–15 answers will vary

RS4
1 600
2 900
3 700
4 800
5 900
6 600
7 400
8 500
9 200
10 100
11–20 answers will vary

RS6
1 $\frac{1}{4}$
2 $\frac{1}{3}$
3 $\frac{1}{5}$
4 $\frac{3}{4}$
5 $\frac{1}{2}$
6 $\frac{2}{3}$
7 $\frac{2}{5}$
8 $\frac{1}{3}$
9 $\frac{3}{4}$

RS9

A
1 130
2 1 200
3 800
4 110
5 1 400
6 600
7 90
8 600
9 80
10 200
11 700
12 80
13 110
14 600
15 800

B
1 81
2 53
3 108
4 126
5 29
6 551
7 563
8 9 236
9 16
10 63
11 77
12 215
13 3 268
14 73
15 38

C
1 542
2 8 462
3 591
4 2 998
5 797
6 5 429
7 9
8 17
9 3
10 1 237
11 5 991
12 5 000
13 103
14 18
15 1 406

D
1 81
2 35
3 83
4 56
5 35
6 54
7 81
8 58
9 83
10 63
11 23
12 80
13 14
14 56
15 80

RS10
1 50
2 80
3 50
4 130
5 80
6 70
7 50
8 1 000
9 800
10 1 000
11 700
12 1 600
13 1 200
14 600
15 900
16 500
17 400
18 600
19 600
20 800
21 700
22 70
23 36
24 400

RS12
1 83
2 66
3 56
4 40
5 42
6 95
7 97
8 565
9 5 592
10 64
11 700
12 24
13 610
14 591
15 42
16 13
17 79

18 79
19 45
20 74
21 53
22 92
23 446
24 48

RS13
1 622
2 324
3 9 330
4 289
5 1 244
6 4
7 694
8 6
9 702
10 4 992
11 519
12 6 428
13 3 223
14 8
15 8
16 17
17 8
18 6 986
19 7 002
20 8 989
21 3 305
22 7 993
23 3 998
24 3 986

RS15
1 52
2 295
3 600
4 433
5 18
6 57

RS16
1 474
2 561
3 541
4 £6.81
5 £6.13
6 303
7 223
8 £2.33
9 £5.90
10 £9.75

RS17
1 259
2 337
3 477
4 676
5 279
6 £6.04

7 £4.78
8 £7.37
9 £3.37
10 £2.67

RS21

1 7 2
2 9
3 8 3
4 4 4
5 3 6
6 18

RS23

1 2× facts include: 6 × 2 = 12, 1 × 2 = 2, 12 × 2 = 24, 11 × 2 = 22, 8 × 2 = 16, 9 × 2 = 18, 10 × 2 = 20, 2 × 2 = 4, 5 × 2 = 10
2 3× facts include: 4 × 3 = 12, 8 × 3 = 24, 6 × 3 = 18, 11 × 3 = 33, 10 × 3 = 30, 5 × 3 = 15, 9 × 3 = 27
3 4× facts include: 3 × 4 = 12, 8 × 4 = 32, 7 × 4 = 28, 10 × 4 = 40, 6 × 4 = 24, 4 × 4 = 16, 2 × 4 = 8, 5 × 4 = 20, 1 × 4 = 4, 9 × 4 = 36
4 5× facts include: 1 × 5 = 5, 11 × 5 = 55, 8 × 5 = 40, 4 × 5 = 20, 6 × 5 = 30, 2 × 5 = 10, 3 × 5 = 15, 12 × 5 = 60, 10 × 5 = 50, 7 × 5 = 35
5 10× facts: 8 × 10 = 80, 10 × 10 = 100, 9 × 10 = 90, 4 × 10 = 40, 7 × 10 = 70, 2 × 10 = 20, 3 × 10 = 30, 1 × 10 = 10, 6 × 10 = 60, 5 × 10 = 50
6 19 29 17 37 1 31
 7 23 13 11
7 Answers could include: all the numbers are odd and there are no odd answers in the 2, 4 or 10 times tables; none of the numbers end in 5 or a zero, so cannot be in the 5 or 10 times tables.

RS24

1 4
2 18
3 8
4 9
5 20
6 12
7 12
8 25
9 3
10 5
11 10
12 5
13 90
14 12
15 50
16 2
17 5
18 100
19 34
20 45
21 7
22 2
23 7
24 10

RS25

1 5 9 1 4 10
2 5 3 9 2 10
3 8 18 11 7 9
4 4
5 3
6 4

RS28

1 1 000
2 123 132 213 231 321
3 30
4 92

RS29

1 148
2 7 hours 55 minutes
3 2 kg 500 g or 2.5 kg
4 980 ml

RS30

1 $10\frac{1}{2}$ litres
2 1.25 litres
3 2.43 km
4 700 g

RS31

1 6.5 cm
2 8 cm
3 9.3 cm
4 10 cm
5 10 cm
6 9.5 cm
7 15 cm
8 16.4 cm

RS32

1 8 km
2 4.5 litres
3 8 days
4 0.74 metre

RS33

1

4

2

5

3 none

6

Written test 1

P >
1 100 150 300 950
    500 900 400 500
2 < > = =
3 a. $\frac{1}{2}$ **b.** $\frac{3}{8}$ **c.** $\frac{5}{6}$ **d.** $\frac{1}{4}$ **e.** $\frac{3}{6}$ $\frac{4}{8}$ $\frac{5}{10}$
4 a. 70   **b.** 1 200   **c.** 913   **d.** 567
  e. 500   **f.** 5 997   **g.** 17   **h.** 70
  i. 130   **j.** 1 300   **k.** 78   **l.** 36
  m. 954   **n.** 5 424   **o.** 17
5 £8.17   £1.19
6 20 16 10 25 21
    18 3 7 5 10
7 10 7 10 27 18
    9 24 5 6 2
8 4
9 1 500 m   650 g   200 ml
10 Has 6 equal sides – hexagon
   Has 4 right angles and 4 equal sides – square
   Is an irregular triangle – scalene triangle
   Has 5 angles, 2 are right angles, and 1 line of symmetry – irregular pentagon
   Has 3 sides, 1 right angle and 1 line of symmetry – isosceles triangle
   Opposite sides are the same length – rectangle
   Is curved – circle
11 6

Written test 2

P 90
1 < > > > = >
2 100 40 20 50 50
    500 600 300 900 900
3 a. 3 buttons should be shaded
  b. 2 squares should be shaded
  c. 3 segments of pizza should be shaded
  d. 2 whole circles and 1 segment of the third should be shaded
  e. $\frac{2}{6}$
4 a. 50   **b.** 900   **c.** 76   **d.** 566
  e. 200   **f.** 3 995   **g.** 15   **h.** 48
  i. 120   **j.** 800   **k.** 35   **l.** 63
  m. 475   **n.** 5 455   **n.** 91
5 701 389
6 16 4 10 21 9
    5 10 2 20 100
7 6 4 5 8 24
    6 9 5 24 2
8 2
9 5   2 litres   700 g
10 4   2   rectangle

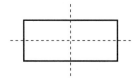

11 44

Mental mathematics test 1

P 80
1 40
2 <
3 26
4 62
5 21
6 32
7 9
8 1
9 37
10 700
11 6 500 metres
12 a
13 120
14 50 g
15 £8
16 900
17 9
18 17
19 b
20 £1.25

Mental mathematics test 2

P ×
1 <
2 970
3 600
4 58
5 24
6 2
7 8
8 400
9 62
10 47
11 $\frac{3}{4}$
12 1 250
13 58 km
14

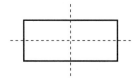

15 46
16 13 hours 20 minutes
17 5
18 $\frac{5}{8}$
19 $\frac{2}{3}$
20 13